THE BOOKSHELF

THE BOOKSHELF

A Potpourri of Stories

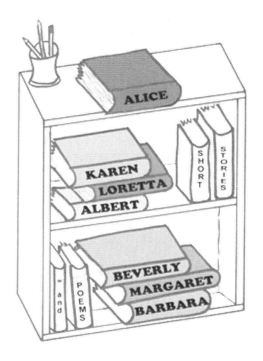

By

The Bookshelf Writers

Volume II

2011

These stories are works of fiction. Any references to historical events; to real people, living or dead; or to locales are intended to give the fiction a setting in historical reality. Other names, characters, places, or incidents are the product of the authors' imaginations and their resemblance to real-life counterparts is entirely coincidental. An occasional story or poem is based on actual people, places and happenings.

Cover and internal design by Barbara J. Bina and Alice Ann Ross.

This book was printed in the United States of America.

To order additional copies of this book, contact:
Xlibris Corporation
1-888-795-4274
www.Xlibris.com
Orders@Xlibris.com
96368

Table of Contents

Alice Ann Ross 7

Karen Saxon 51

Loretta Walker 57

Albert E. Farrar Jr. 81

Beverly Anderson 113

Margaret Watland 153

Barbara J. Bina 183

Alice's Stories

Alice Ann Ross

Alice was born and raised in Detroit Michigan, but has lived in Washington State for the past fifty years. She says that qualifies her as a true *Washingtonian*. She started and leads a writer's workshop called *The Bookshelf Writers*, in Puyallup, Washington.

Music and her three sons were the focal point of Alice's life until she could no longer play her beloved violin and wondered what she would do without music. For Alice, writing was the answer.

From an early age, she wrote speeches and essays, but never fiction. She wrote her first short story six years ago and hasn't stopped writing since. *Valerie, Letters to God*, a novella, was published in the spring of 2010. She continues to write in her favorite form—short stories.

Alice has included in this book a sampling of different genres from her writings for your enjoyment.

The Legend of Alistair McCarthy

By
Alice Ann Ross

Great Uncle Alistair was our legend. Even his name lent to the mythical qualities of fable. Alistair means *Helper of God* and our surname, McCarthy, means *Loving Person.* It fit Uncle Alistair perfectly, they said.

The telling of Great Uncle Alistair's story was anticipated by the children of the McCarthy family every year on All Hallow's Eve. The story, when first told, was a true account of kindness. No one knows how or when this story became a tradition. Where truth ends and fiction begins is unclear, but the McCarthy children believed every word.

Great Grandmother McCarthy told the story to the wee ones every year until her death. Grandmother Ada is now the teller of the tale.

XXXXXX

It was cold that night. The wind howled on the moors. All of Ireland hungered. The potato crop had failed once again. Alistair was stoking the fire when a great gust of wind swept down the chimney and the meager fire sputtered a second, then snuffed out. The only light came from the moon through the little window of his thatched hut.

In the wind he heard a voice calling, "Alistair, help them, help them."

What was that, he wondered? He ran outside to see if he could hear the voice again.

"Alistair, help them, help them," he heard once more and at the same time, he saw a line of stars falling downward in an arc then circling a spot high on the hillside.

Shivering, he ran back inside and crawled under the covers on his small cot to ward off the chill and the frightening sounds. The wind continued to wail. It whipped around the corners of the small house and still he heard, "Alistair, help them, help them." He jumped off the bed and railed his arms towards the ceiling.

"What do you want of me?" he cried.

"Go to the place of the stars."

The voice must mean the stars that hovered on the tor, he thought. He went outside and saw the circle of stars half way up the mountain. Suddenly a small whirlwind formed at the corner of the woods and moved stealthily toward him. He was so terrified, he couldn't move. It came closer until it stood five feet from him and spun faster and faster. At the peak of its velocity a word spewed from its midst. "GO!" it said and immediately dissipated.

What did it mean? How could he help anyone? He lost everything in the famine. What could he do? Was the voice in the wind telling him of people's hunger? He knew most families were needy, as was he, but all he had was the bag of starter-potatoes he held back to begin next year's crop. If they were lost, the following year would be bleaker than this year

Alistair went back to bed. He fantasized about more prosperous and happy times and tried to sleep. The storm worsened. Thunder rolled, lightening flashed and the wind was at an unbelievable pitch.

"GO! Help them!" he heard once more.

With that, Alistair could stand no more. He leapt from bed, threw on his warmest clothes and flew out the door. He needed to find out what was up there under the circle of stars. When he got to the edge of the woods he stopped, turned, ran back to his root cellar and grabbed the treasured bag of seed-potatoes.

Following the path up the mountain, he headed to the point where the stars floated. He finally arrived at the door of a small hovel. Alistair raised his hand, but the door opened before he could knock and a young boy stood there smiling.

"We were waiting for ye," he said. "We knew ye would come."

The room glowed from a small fire in an open stove. Alistair looked across the room to a bed that held the most beautiful woman he'd ever seen and in her arms was a newborn babe.

"'Tis me baby sister," the young lad told him. "Her name is Siobhán. We prayed ye would come. Did ye bring food?"

"Oh yes," said Great Uncle Alistair without hesitation. "I've brought ye potatoes."

XXXXXX

Thus it was that your Great Uncle Alistair helped save the life of Saint Siobhán. It was half way up a mountain on All Hallow's Eve. He came with a bag of his precious potatoes.

The famine ended the following year.

Place Poem

small, cold, bare
austere
looking sadly paltry
from the silence
into the din
shuddering walls
never-ending wind

Alistair's Thatched Hut on the Moor

The Danny and Mark Mysteries

Ghost-man with the White Eye

By
Alice Ann Ross

"Holy cow! Did you see that?" Danny asked his best buddy Mark.

"What? I didn't see anything."

"Just look. Can't you see him in the window?"

The boys were standing at the end of the neighbor's driveway.

Mark tilted his head toward the house next-door and stared intently. "Oh yeah, now I see him. He's kind of creepy. Who do you think he is?"

"I don't know, but I'm gonna find out. Oh my gosh, he's coming out. Run!" Danny said.

They darted behind the hedge that ran along Danny's driveway and watched as the man came out and walked toward his car. He looked like a scarecrow with white skin and hair. His hair looked like a messy marshmallow. The thing that startled them most was his eyes. One eye was a light faded grey and looked white, like his hair. The other eye was light green. Danny and Mark agreed he looked like a ghost—a ghost-man with a white eye. The Ghost-man backed out of his driveway and drove toward town.

Maybe he and Mark could find out something about this guy. As soon as the neighbor was out of sight, Danny and Mark went to look in the basement windows. In the dim light, they could just make out a painting leaning against the wall.

"That's the dumbest picture I ever saw. Who would want something like that?" Mark asked.

With nothing more to see, they went back to Danny's house.

"Hi Mark!" Danny's mother called from upstairs. Would you like to stay for dinner? Maybe you could spend the night."

After dinner, the boys went to Danny's room to plan the events of the *Danny and Mark Detective Agency*.

"We'll have to wait until Ghost-man leaves before we can go back over there tomorrow," Mark said.

Danny and Mark decided to push the bunk bed next to the window. If anything happened next-door in the night, they'd hear it.

It was around 2:00 a.m. when Mark sat straight up in bed and banged his head on the ceiling. He forgot he was on the top bunk. "What was that?" he whispered.

"Don't know. I heard it too," Danny said.

They got on their knees, one on the top bunk and one on the lower, and pressed their faces against the window. If someone looked up, he would have seen two ten-year-old heads, one above the other, peering out. It didn't occur to them that they could be clearly seen in the bright moonlight.

What they saw was peculiar. There was a black van in the driveway and a guy taking something from Ghost-man. He gave the Ghost-man an envelope and drove away.

Ghost-man turned and those strange eyes looked up at Danny's house. Both boys dove under the covers and didn't come out until morning.

After breakfast, the two *detectives* circled the block, avoiding the house next door and headed up to Ryan Road. When they approached the woods, they smelled something awful.

"Eeeew!" Danny said holding his nose. "What stinks? I knew it. They've got dead bodies back here."

They were just about to walk into the woods when they heard someone shout, "What are you kids doing back there? Get out if you know what's good for you."

Danny turned on his heel and ran as fast as he could with Mark right behind him. When they got back to Danny's house, they shot through the door and Mr. Murray put his hands out and said, "What's the big hurry? What have you two been up to?"

"Dad," Danny said, breathless. "Something bad is going on next door."

"It was really scary," Mark said and nodded his head in agreement.

"Now you boys leave that man alone. He's entitled to his privacy," Danny's father said. "You don't know anything anyway. Find something else to do besides bothering the neighbors."

Dejected, Danny and Mark climbed the stairs to Danny's room.

Later Mrs. Murray came to the door and told Mark his mother phoned and wanted him home.

"I'll ride my bike over tomorrow and we can go to the woods again," Mark said. "Maybe we'll be able to go in there if those men aren't around. I hope we don't get killed. See you tomorrow."

The next day was Sunday and Danny woke up to howling wind and rain. Oh no! Now we won't be able to check out the woods and tomorrow is the first day of school. Rats!

XXXXXX

With soccer season starting, homework to be done and boy scouts getting back into gear, the neighbor's woods were forgotten for a while.

One Saturday that fall Danny and Mark rode down Ryan Road to Tulia's Drug Store. Mr. Murray gave them money to get a treat. As they approached the woods, they smelled that terrible stink again and remembered the terrifying neighbor. When Danny glanced to his right, he saw Ghost-man coming through the trees. The Ghost-man saw him too, stopped and stared. Danny kept riding but couldn't take his eyes off the man. He ran smack-dab into a tree, bent his front wheel, flew off the bike, and scraped his arm.

Mark jumped off his bike and came running, "You okay? What the heck were you doing?"

"I was watching Ghost-man," Danny grumbled.

"I didn't see him. Are you sure?"

"Of course I'm sure. I'm not crazy! Oh gads, look at my bike. My dad's going to kill me."

Mr. Murray arrived home that evening, crossed the porch to the front door and immediately noticed the bike. Inside he called out, "Danny, where are you? Are you all right?"

"Yes Dad," Danny said as he shuffled into the front room

"You want to tell me about the bike?"

"Well, Mark and I were riding up Ryan Road and Ghost-man came out of the woods. I was looking at him and I just, sort of, kind of—ran into a tree."

"Where you spying on the neighbor again? I thought I told you to leave him alone."

"No dad, I wasn't. Mark and I were riding to the drug store to get a *Super-Duper-Gigantic Banana Split* at Tulia's when Ghost-man walked out of the woods. He just stared at me and that's when I hit the tree. We weren't spying, but I still think something weird is happening over there."

"I don't want you to even think about the man next door. Forget it! Is that clear?"

The next night Danny read a comic book while his mom and dad watched the news on TV. Danny glanced up and saw something he thought he recognized on the screen.

"What was that?" he yelled.

"Must you be so loud?" His mother asked. "It was a painting that was stolen in Austria and is worth $10,000,000.00."

"It was in Ghost-man's house! Mark and I saw it in his basement. Why is it worth so much? It's the ugliest thing I've ever seen."

"Are you sure?" Mr. Murray asked.

"Am I sure it's ugly?"

"No, are you sure it's the same painting?"

"Oh Yeah! It was leaning against the wall in the basement."

It was all finally coming together for Mr. Murray, the need for privacy, packages in the middle of the night. Could Ghost-man be an art thief?

"Can you beat that?" Mr. Murray said. "I guess I owe you and Mark an apology. I really thought your imaginations were out of control."

XXXXXX

"I looked for the painting on the Internet and found out this painting was stolen from a museum in Austria," Danny's father told the police captain. "This guy's real name is Ernst Adolph Spritzenhour. They showed his picture. He's wanted over there too, for stealing art." Mr. Murray continued.

"Are you're sure it's the same guy?" Captain Dudley asked.

"Captain," Mr. Murray said. "Can you possibly think there would be two faces like that on the planet?"

"Dad, tell Captain Dudley about the stinky smells."

"Oh that," the captain said. "Some people were using the corner of that property as a dumping ground. When it gets warm, it really smells foul. I thought we'd put a stop to that. Looks like I'll have to get tough and issue some fines."

A few hours later, the police were at the neighbor's house. They banged on the front door. Danny and Mark charged up the stairs, pushed the bunk bed over to the window again and took their places, one on top and one below. They could witness everything from there.

The police went inside and soon came out leading Ghost-man away in handcuffs.

XXXXXX

The Sunday News carried a picture of Danny and Mark on the front page and the article called them "local heroes."

Danny Murray and Mark Swanson talked about that summer for years.

The old farmhouse was taken down and the city made the acreage into a neighborhood park. They called it—*Murray Square*.

Two Points of View

The Blind Date—View One

Hers

By
Alice Ann Ross

His name was Fergus Doppelhanger from Husker-Hollow, which should have given me my first clue. He owned the biggest chicken ranch in Tennessee and was one of Irene's major clients. Irene and I have been best friends since kindergarten. She's an attorney in corporate law and represents Mr. Doppelhanger's interests here in Washington. Irene said he loved western movies and anything to do with the old west.

"Come on Carol, he'll only be here for one night. Jerry and I would go with you, but we have an important business dinner to attend, besides, you need to get out more and though I hate to bring this up, you owe me a favor."

"Okay, okay! I'll do it, but this makes us even," I said emphatically.

As I was leaving, Irene called after me, "He said to be casual."

xxxxxx

This can't be it, I thought. The building looked like something out of a John Wayne movie. Irene said to dress casual, but this was ridiculous. I pulled into the parking lot and double-checked the address. 71926 Pacific Highway South was the right address, but it was a tavern! Irene knows I don't drink and I've never been in this kind of establishment in my life. I looked down at my pretty, casual red dress and pulled the matching shawl tighter around my shoulders.

I reluctantly walked into the tavern. Immediately the odor of stale beer and cigarette smoke assaulted my nose. A hush came over the place as the door closed behind me. I wanted to be fashionably late, but it occurred to me the word *fashion*able had no correlation to this place whatsoever. When my eyes adjusted to the dim lighting, I saw two pool tables off to one side and a few round tables and chairs strewn about. The bar against the wall was huge. Two men and a woman sat there and stared at me.

The bartender called out as I made my way to a table at the back of the room, "What'll it be, lady?" I ordered a glass of iced tea to have something to do while I waited. I sat down; not realizing the bartender usually didn't serve people at their table. He brought my tea and put it down heavily. Tea sloshed over the top of the glass. He walked away and mumbled something about being a damned waitress.

I watched every man that came in the front door and the knot in my stomach grew.

Why had I let Irene talk me into this?

First through the door was a man seven feet, ten inches tall who weighed approximately ninety pounds. He looked like Ichabod Crane.

"Hey there, pretty lady," the tall skinny man yelled at me. "Ain't you the cutest thing?" All eyes were on my red face.

Please, if there's a God up there, don't let him be my date, I thought and shuddered. I was relieved when Ichabod took a seat at the bar.

I am going to kill Irene.

Then a man shaped like a Sumo Wrestler came through the door dressed in jeans three sizes too small that hung precariously below his ample belly. He wore an old sweatshirt with the arms cut out. Oh no, please, I thought.

I visualized Irene's head in the guillotine.

Someone tapped me on the shoulder from behind and said in a deep voice, "Are you Carol Owens, by any chance?" Putting on my most dazzling smile, I turned and said, "Why yes, I am."

xxxxxx

They've cloned Count Dracula and put him in western garb! Before me was a diminutive man with dyed jet-black hair and long sideburns.

He had little dark pig's eyes and a huge hooked nose. His mouth was a straight line—no lips! He wore a black cowboy hat and a rawhide vest. The leather fringe was over the top, even for this place.

"It's nice to meet you," he said. "My name's Fergus Doppelhanger and I've been looking forward to this."

I thought I was adult enough not to care about a man's looks. Apparently not!

The date went downhill from there. He bragged incessantly about his many conquests with women back in Tennessee and proudly told of the life-sized stuffed clown he'd won at the fair last week for sharp shooting. He even brought a picture to show me. The clown was seven feet tall and brashly stood in the corner of Fergus's living room. Now that's what I'd call class!

After almost falling asleep, I decided enough time had elapsed to leave graciously.

Never again, I vowed!

Someone ought to warn Irene her life was in danger. If I killed Irene for this, do you think I'd be acquitted?

The Blind Date—View Two

His

This was my favorite watering hole in the state of Washington and I figured she'd love it. I came in the back door and motioned to Jake, the bartender, to ask if my date was there yet. Jake pointed to a woman who sat alone at a table near the back window. Her back was turned to me. Is that really her, I wondered? What a dish!

I'm glad I decided to re-dye my hair. I looked pretty good in my new western vest with the leather trim if I do say so myself.

Irene must have forgotten to tell her to dress casual. She's all gussied up.

We talked over dinner, but I did most of the talking. She didn't say much. Whoopee! Finally, I've met a gal who likes to listen. I know I impressed her with stories about my winning ways with the ladies and I think she was flabbergasted with my sharp-shooting ability.

I was disappointed when she told me she had to leave early. I said, "I'm awful sorry you have to go so soon. I thought we could go bowling, but you're not exactly dressed for bowling, are you? How 'bout we go by your place so you can change your duds?"

"Oh I don't think so. Thanks anyway."

"Are you sure you don't want to go bowling?"

"No thank you. I'd better get home," she said. "Thanks for the chili-dog."

"Yeah, they make the best dogs here, outside of Tennessee," I told her.

All eyes in the place were on her as she walked through the room and out the front door. I was proud as a hen with a newborn chick!

XXXXXX

What a great date. Everyone in the joint was jealous, especially Slim Jim.

I think she really dug me. Maybe we could go to the Demolition Derby the next time I'm in town.

I'll have to remember to thank Irene for my super-duper date with Carol.

Mauri of the Moors

By
Alice Ann Ross

They broke through the door of the hut with swords drawn. Mauri's mother pushed her out a small opening at the back of the room. The strange men were occupied subduing her husband.

She whispered, "Run little Mauri. Go to the Moors and hide in the heather. Hurry!"

Later in the day, after they took her family from her, Mauri, with aching heart, came back to the cottage. Everything looked the same except now she was alone and time had no meaning. Night after night, she cried herself to sleep.

Mauri made peace with her loneliness and began singing again the songs her mother taught her.

The cottage was up the tor from the quiet valley below. From the yard, the view was breathtaking. A small lake in the distance dominated the vista. Mauri's moor was in the high rainfall region characterized by heavy fog and mist. At night, the moors were sinister.

One night Mauri went onto the moors and gathered stones to build a cairn in honor of her parents. She instinctively knew they would not return and wanted a place to come to remember. How many years had it been? She never wondered any more.

It was summer on this evening and a ghostly mist covered the lowlands. Mauri stepped outside as the sun was setting. This was the only time of day she could walk to the cairn that commemorated her family. She took flowers and placed them at the base of the stones. The flowers grew in the garden behind the house and Mauri tended them, but only after sunset. Her parents told her to never go outside alone during daylight.

During the daytime hours there were many inside chores to be done. She made bread as best she could from watching her mother. It wasn't as good, but it satisfied her hunger. Stew was started with the venison in the larder and the vegetables from the garden. The dirt floor needed to be swept and water carried from the cistern in a wooden bucket every night.

The upland moors got very windy and boggy when it rained. The walk to the cairn was an unpleasant journey most of the time. The fog was so dense Mauri could barely see five feet in front of her and the bog came almost to her knees, but she continued to her destination and placed her flowers, as she knew she should.

The years passed, but Mauri didn't notice. She didn't notice she never changed or grew into a woman. She didn't know this was the norm. It never occurred to her that every day was the same as the day before. The meat in the larder hadn't lessened. The flour stayed at the same level and the flowers never wilted.

She wasn't happy. She wasn't sad. She merely was.

One day while Mauri was making bread, she was conscious of something different in her world. There were strange noises coming from the lowlands. At first, she thought it was the wind. Then there was the honking. Maybe it's geese, she thought, but it didn't sound like geese she'd heard before. After hearing this din for days, Mauri defied the warnings of her parents long ago and stepped outside into the sunshine. The sun was very bright she thought, as she squinted. When her eyes adjusted to the dazzling light, she walked toward the edge of the tor to look out over the valley.

In Mauri's mind, the Vikings had kidnapped her parents four days ago and the last time she looked down into the valley was the day before that.

She could not comprehend what her eyes beheld. Now she could see what was making the strange noises, but had no idea what these things were. In the valley there were paths made of something black and hard. Little things made of metal sped back and forth at high-speeds on the strange black paths.

She realized the noises she'd heard emanated from these objects and she was afraid.

Ten-year-old Mauri turned and ran back as quickly as she could to her familiar cottage. Her heart was beating so fast and hard, it hurt. Through the front door and straight to the larder she went to get a piece of venison and water from the wooden bucket. She started the stew for the day as she had for time untold.

Her parents had been abducted in the year 1025. For Mauri, her point in time remained the same—1025.

XXXXX

"Hey Angus! Get up here slowpoke. Get a load of this," Ian said.

"I'm coming," chubby Angus puffed. "What's got you so excited?"

"I think I found some ancient ruin," Ian said excitedly.

"Gosh," Angus said. "It looks like some old house even though the roof is gone. Hey look! What do you think this is?"

"It looks like a piece of an old wooden bucket."

The year was 2010.

The Parable of King Fu Cha-Cha

By
Alice Ann Ross

These three stories are dedicated to my niece,
Nancy Kay Kiviaho Swistok, with love.

King Fu Cha-Cha and the Long-tailed Warbler

King Fu Cha-Cha lived in a country far away called ChirPing. King Fu Cha-Cha was a very good King!

The birds of this land made the most beautiful music in the world. The king's favorite song was that of the Long-tailed Warbler. One Long-tailed Warbler sang the best of all. He named his special little bird Lei-Lei. Every morning he would go to his door and call, "Come little friend Lei-Lei. Come, sing for me."

One day King Fu Cha-Cha called and called but the woods were quiet. The next morning he called Lei-Lei again, but still no answer.

The servants from the palace searched and people from the village hunted for Lei-Lei, but she had disappeared. King Fu Cha-Cha tended to his duties that day, but was worried about his little feathered friend.

Later, in the evening, a man from the village brought him a small box. He told King Fu Cha-Cha that his little friend with the most beautiful song had died. King Fu Cha-Cha felt truly sad. He called upon his friends to come help him say goodbye. They buried Lei-Lei in a little clearing near the woods. On a large rock they wrote:

Lei-Lei the Long-tailed Warbler
Friend of King Fu Cha-Cha
With the most beautiful song of all!

The Lost Little Girl

Now, King Fu Cha-Cha was a good king who wanted all the people in his kingdom to be happy.

One day, the king was making plans for a birthday party for Queen Fu Chi-Chi when the head mistress of the school came running in.

"One of my students has run off into the woods," she said. "I know My-lin is an unhappy child because she misses her parents so much and it is hard for her to study. I was upset with My-lin for daydreaming today. I guess I raised my voice when I said, 'My-lin, stop dreaming and do your lesson.' This upset little My-lin so much she ran out of the school."

My-lin ran through the school grounds and right into the woods. She ran and ran, crying the whole time. Soon My-lin was very tired. She found a place under a tree to rest before starting back to the school.

She fell asleep and by the time she woke up, it was getting dark.

When she got up and looked around, every direction looked the same. Which way should she go? It was getting darker and darker.

She was lost!

My-lin was scared and cold and she cried herself to sleep again. She thought she heard voices. When she opened her eyes, there lying beside her, was a fawn keeping her warm while she slept. My-lin sat up and saw the fawn's mother watching them. The voices she heard got closer and louder.

"Thank you little fawn for keeping me warm," My-lin said. The doe nodded and led her baby away from the approaching men.

One man saw My-lin and yelled, "She's here! She's here!" Everyone was so glad. They wrapped My-lin in a blanket and took her to see King Fu Cha-Cha.

"Why did you run away?" The king asked. "Are you that unhappy?"

"No! I was just thinking about home and when the mistress spoke loudly, she scared me," My-lin whimpered. "I really was just sad and wanted my mother."

The king told My-lin he had a surprise for her and slowly turned her around.

My-lin yelled, "Momma! Papa! I am so sorry I worried you and all the people. I know I was wrong and I will never run away again!

The Door in the Garden Wall

King Fu Cha-Cha walked in his garden one sunny morning thinking about the baby soon to be born. The flowers smelled sweet and he heard the song of the birds. He thought about how his life will change with a baby in the palace.

As the king strolled that morning, he noticed a door in the garden wall that he had not seen before.

"What is this?" He wondered. "How could I have not noticed this door before?"

He went to the door and pulled on the handle. At first it did not move. He pulled harder and the door slowly opened.

What stood beyond the door should have been the road around the palace and across the road he should have seen the familiar woods, but that is not what the king saw.

King Fu Cha-Cha saw a long hallway, which was quite dark. He could not see to its end. He wondered if he should enter. He decided to step inside and as soon as he did, the door slammed behind him. He tried to re-open the door. This time no matter how hard he pulled on it, the door wouldn't budge. There was no other way to go so he started down the long hall.

After walking for a while, he thought he heard the sound of children and at the end of the hall, he saw light. The king hurried toward the light and sounds. When he walked out of the dark hall, he found himself in the most wonderful playground. It was full of brightly colored playthings.

There were red swings and blue slides. There was a merry-go-round and great huge balls. There was a cotton candy stall and candy apples. There were clowns and play cars. There was a red train full of the village children and driving the train was the most handsome lad the king had ever seen.

Wait a minute, the king thought. Was that a crown on the driver's head? Yes! Yes, it was a golden crown."

The children were all singing, "Hooray for Prince Fu Cha-Chi! Hooray for Prince Fu Cha-Chi!"

"It's a sign," he thought. "I am going to have a son and the entire kingdom will love him."

He walked into the dark hall and back to the door in the garden wall. He was home again and was now certain the baby would be a boy.

Immediately, he started making plans to build a wonderful playground for the village children like the one he had just seen at the end of the dark hall.

Then the king ran into the palace shouting for the queen. He couldn't wait to tell her what he had seen beyond the garden wall and the news that their baby was to be a boy.

"Fu Chi-Chi," he called. "I have news for you. We are going to have a son!

A new king will be born!"

The Pinnacle

By
Alice Ann Ross

Our turn to go to the *Pinnacle* was tomorrow. Each family was assigned one day a year to venture up there to see the sky. It was considered quite an event and we looked forward to it with great anticipation. The *Pinnacle* was the summit of the building and the only access to a vision of the sky. We heard the sight was amazing at night when you could see the stars, but we were never assigned a night visit.

I jumped from my bed early, excited to see the sky today. The light from the sky was very different from the artificial illumination we knew. It was always a spectacular sight with interesting things to do while at the *Pinnacle*. Screens were set up with history lessons, music, games and one whole side of the *Pinnacle* was made into a man-made lake and beach. We played on the sand much the same as our ancestors. We learned this in our history *book/screens*.

Many other families were scheduled at the same time. I hoped Lamuna would be there. My parents and I frolicked and played for our allotted time. Our special day sadly came to a close. We packed our things and took our memories with us until next year. I never saw Lamuna.

History *book/screens* told of a time when people lived in individual houses and walked under the sun and sky, but that was eons ago. The pictures in the archives showed people actually enjoyed the sun, but the sun became our enemy hundreds of years ago when the protective ozone layer was damaged and humans were forced to go *Inside*.

The earth was running out of space for human habitation when the *Great Ailing* began. People all over the globe became ill. Physicians discovered that the sun was the cause. Technology became advanced to the point it could take structures up into the clouds. My ancestors could never imagine the building in which I live. This building is attached to many others and they reached miles up from the ground. Each group of buildings constituted a city housing thousands of people. There were similar structures all over the planet. It was impossible for me to conceive a time before man moved *Inside*.

I read an ancient book once, about a family with twelve children . . . unheard of in our society. The book was called *Cheaper by the Dozen* and it sounded dreadful. With so many people in one home, they must have crawled all over each other. The children were called siblings. What an odd concept. The law now limits a couple to one child and that's only if they were lucky enough to be granted a permit.

My friend Arno lived in a different *city/building*. We talked on the *tele-comunicator* at times, but I've never *touch-met* him. It's rare to *touch-meet* a person from another *city/building*. Friendships were through *tele-com*.

XXXXXX

My mother and father worked in the laboratory where they made sustenance. Food came in the form of tablets. I understood that in ages past, food was consumed by chewing and swallowing. Our tablets came in various categories. If we chose a pill labeled strawberries, once it got to the stomach, it sent a message to the brain and we actually tasted strawberries, a pleasant sensation. The same held true for the tastes handed down through the centuries for all our *taste-desires*. We were taught what the food items looked like in our *book/screens*, but I've never seen or touched a strawberry or steak or any other food. Today my *taste-desire* was for watermelon and steak. Every day we chose an item from four lists (one from each list) for nutritional/health purposes. We also went to the track to run or walk for an hour every day. It was mandatory to stay fit.

Each *city/building* was divided into quadrants and run separately. Our quadrant planned a concert on the newly installed *Pipe-a-musique*. It was the biggest one ever built and the sound should be fabulous. Huge pipes hung down from the rafters. The pipes were remotely connected to three keyboards placed around the arena. The best virtuosos on the *Pipe-a-musique* were hired. The music to be played is by a composer from the *Primitive Era*. The compositions were recently found hidden in a cave on the *Outside*. The long-lost composer's name is Andrew Lloyd-Webber. The work is called *Phantom of the Opera*. His scores were hundreds of years old and very fragile when found. It should be a wonderful concert. Everyone loved the *Pipe-a-musique*.

XXXXXX

My name is Narvak. It comes from my father's name Narvold and my mother's name Vaktel. Next month will be my nineteenth birthday. I haven't told my parents, but I know a young woman I would like to take as my mate. Her name is Lamuna. We ride the *Tube-rail* together to and from school in the Main Quadrant. I heard rumors that a mate was chosen for me by my parents and a government official. This way of choosing a partner for offspring has lasted far too long. Most young people in this year of 2512 were ready to rebel. It was time to tell my parents about my feelings for Lamuna.

This evening when we returned from our run, I said, "Mother and Father, there is something I need to propose to you. I have chosen a mate and want you to consent to our being *united*."

"This can not be," my father expressed. "We made arrangements for you to be united with the daughter of our friends Muva and Jorgel. You remember Mujor, don't you son?"

"Yes, of course I remember Mujor, but I love Lamuna. No one ever speaks of love anymore."

"Now Novak, you know it was discovered long ago that love was an unnecessary emotion and only caused unrest in people. It is not recommended. I suggest you bury this point of view immediately," my mother said coldly.

"Mother, you and I both know that never worked. Some people always insisted on living with affection and I am one of them. There are lots of young people today who are ready to fight for love as part of our lives."

"That's just the talk of youth," my mother said. "It's dangerous talk. Besides, no permit will be given to you and that's final."

I knew I could never convince my parents to think as I did. There was only one thing to do and this was discussed in our peer groups many times. We young people would go *Outside*.

XXXXXX

Knowing that the sun would eventually cause sickness and death, Narvak and Lamuna with their friends Arno, his mate Melar and one hundred of their companions left the *city/building* and walked *Outside*. The choice was theirs and they chose to live with love.

Clipper Maid of the Seas

By
Alice Ann Ross

The laundry was folded and preparations for dinner complete. I stood in the doorway to the backyard and breathed in the delicious aroma of freshly mown grass and someone in the area was burning autumn leaves. The combination was heady. Occasionally it occurs to me (most of the time I take it for granted) what an incredibly lovely country this is.

It's a perfect day to take the books to my mother she wanted to borrow. She hasn't been feeling well and maybe the books would be a distraction for her. I have some news to share too. Mom and Daddy were getting older and at times, I forget this. I think of them as indestructible. I think they will always be with me. Then I'll notice that Daddy's back isn't as straight as it should be or how hard it is for Mom to tie her shoes and a little pain touches my heart.

There was plenty of time to ride to their house and get back to make dinner for my husband Charlie. I pulled my bike out of the garage and headed down the lane. As I happily peddled my old bike toward town (I was about a block away from the folk's place.) when I heard a huge explosion. I looked up and saw an enormous fireball drop out of the sky. It landed right on my folk's street. I was so startled by this, I fell off my bike and skinned my knees pretty badly, but I didn't notice until much later.

It was realized afterward that what hit my parent's little lane was the heavy flight engine of the *Clipper Maid of the Seas,* Pan Am flight 103, Wednesday, December 21, 1998. Two hundred fifty-nine people on board all perished plus eleven people on the ground, including my beloved parents. There was nothing left of them to bury.

Lockerbie residents lived for many days with the sight of bodies in their yards and on the streets. They couldn't be moved until the forensic teams photographed and tagged them.

One poor man told of his experience, "A boy was lying at the bottom of the steps on to the road. He was a young laddie with brown socks and blue trousers on. Later that evening my son-in-law asked for a blanket to cover him. I didn't know he was dead. I gave him a lamb's wool travelling rug, thinking it'd keep the lad warm. Two more girls were lying dead across the road, one of them bent over garden railings. It was just as though they were sleeping. The boy lay at the bottom of my stairs for days. Every time I came back to my house for clothes, he was still there. 'My boy is still there,' I used to tell the waiting policeman. Eventually on Saturday, I couldn't take it no more. 'You got to get my boy lifted,' I told the policeman. That night he was moved."

Lockerbie has never forgotten Wednesday, December 21, 1998 and it's a tribute to us that we have kept going.

The books I was taking to my mother that unhappy day are now in a special place on a shelf in my living room surrounded by pictures of her and my father.

xxxxxx

I just learned I was expecting a baby. This was the news I was taking to my mother the tragic day the *Clipper Maid of the Seas* fell from the sky, ten years ago.

xxxxxx

"Mum, I'm hungry," my ten-year-old son Ross said, as though he was in pain and due to die if he didn't get cookies immediately.

"You're always hungry," I laughed.

Life goes on.

An Irish Lullaby

By
Alice Ann Ross

It sounded way off in the distance. Oh stop, I thought. I need my sleep, but it came closer and closer and became louder and louder. Finally, I was forced to open my eyes. The sound was deafening right next to my ear. I glanced at the clock as I grabbed the phone and read 3:46 a.m. Who would be calling at this hour?

"Maura?" The voice said through static on the line.

"Yes, this is Maura," I said sleepily. "Who's calling?"

"It's Sinead," the voice replied.

This can't be good, I thought. My sister wouldn't be calling from Killarney at this hour unless something was wrong.

"What is it?" I asked as I steeled myself for her answer.

"It's Mum," she said through muffled sobs. "Oh Maura! She's really bad."

"No!" I said. "I just talked to her yesterday morning. She said she was feeling better."

"She didn't want you to worry, but the cancer returned months ago. She made us all swear not to tell you."

"My God, Sinead. How could you have agreed to that? I would have come and been with her."

I heard Sinead crying and even though I was upset, I felt bad for her and said, "Don't cry. I'll come over as soon as I can."

When I hung up, I found myself trembling and couldn't stop. I knew my mother was going to die. I don't know how I knew, but I had no doubt.

I went back to the bedroom where my husband was still sleeping. That man could sleep through anything. I lay down next to him, flat on my back and stared at the ceiling. I couldn't even cry.

The next morning I started making plans to fly to Ireland. Jack's mother said she'd come and stay with Jack and the kids. The following day I was on a plane headed to the place where I was born.

On the flight, I tried to sleep, but a song kept running around in my head. *Over in Killarney, many years ago, me mither sang a song to me in tones so sweet and low.*

A flood of memories came, memories of Mum when she was young and I was just a wee thing. She was not happy. Who could be, living with my father?

She often said, "I'm on the verge of a nervous breakdown." She told me I was the cause many times. I didn't know what I had done, but I believed her and tried to be good. It wasn't until my teen years that I realized I never could please her and in one way, I stopped trying. I argued with her and she became infuriated with me.

"Maura why do you always argue? Why can't you be more like Sinead?"

"I argue Mum, when I know you're wrong and I don't want to be like Sinead. I don't even like her," I yelled and was sent to my room once again.

When Sinead got married, Mum cried her eyes out because *her girl* was moving to the other side of Killarney. When I got married and was moving across an ocean to the U.S.—not a tear. I took that to mean she was glad to be rid of me.

When I see her again, I thought, I'm going to tell her how much I've always loved her. Our relationship was such, it didn't lead to words of endearment. She made me angry at times, but my love for her was bottomless. I wanted her to know this and I wanted to hear her say she loved me.

xxxxxx

My father and sister were at the airport to meet me. When I realized my father was driving, I was filled with dread. He was the worst driver since the invention of the automobile.

He always bragged about the time he was stopped for a traffic violation, "That stupid officer told me he'd been following me for six blocks with his lights flashing and I should have pulled over when I saw him in the rear-view mirror. I told him, 'Young man, I keep my eyes on the road. I don't look in those mirrors.'" That one cost him a pretty penny. The frightening thing is, he still thinks he was right.

We arrived at the hospital miraculously and parked. I followed my father and sister through the halls. They had become used to the corridors in the past few weeks. I tried to put myself in control of my emotions, much as I do when I perform. When we arrived at my mother's room there was an orderly posted at her door. He informed us my mother had died a few hours before our arrival.

They tell me I screamed and then went somewhere inside of me. I followed them around but couldn't respond to anyone. The doctor said I had removed myself from the intense sorrow I felt. It was more than an hour before I came back to reality. xxxxxx

I surmised I was 30,000 feet above the Atlantic Ocean when my mother died. Her life had ceased to be while I sat in that plane, but I didn't know. How could I not know? The world did not change with my mother's passing, but I did. I knew I would never hear her say *I love you* or *I was proud of you* or *you were a pretty girl* or any of the things mothers usually say to daughters and the chance to tell her how much I loved her, was gone forever.

My mother loved me in her own way and I have spent forty years trying to forgive her for not telling me.

An Irish Lullaby

Over in Killarney
Many years ago,
Me mither sang a song to me
In tones so sweet and low. Just a simple little ditty,
In her good ould Irish way,
And I'd give the world if she could sing
That song to me this day.

Chorus:
Too-ra-loo-ra-loo-ral, Too-ra-loo-ra-li,
Too-ra-loo-ra-loo-ral, hush now, don't you cry!
Too-ra-loo-ra-loo-ral, Too-ra-loo-ra-li,
Too-ra-loo-ra-loo-ral, that's an Irish Lullaby.

Rhonda's Plan

By
Alice Ann Ross

A sponge carpet of pine needles covered the trail. It cushioned their soles and absorbed the sounds of their footsteps.

Rhonda stopped short and whispered, "Something's coming. There, to the right. It could be a bear!"

"Oh lord! My first camping trip and we're going to be killed," she thought.

"I didn't hear anything," Tom replied.

Rhonda Demming and Thomas Bartlett seemed perfect together. She was a violinist for the Okanogan Symphony and Tom was in his final year studying law and was already offered a position at a large Canadian Financial Group upon graduation.

They met at a small college in Kamloops, B.C. They were the epitome of the cliché, *opposites attract*. Everything seemed perfect.

Rhonda started playing the violin at an early age and as soon as she could read words, she read everything she saw. She drove the family nutty. She read street signs. She read cereal boxes. One time when she was four, she read in the newspaper that Santa was a fairy tale. She told all her little friends that Santa Claus wasn't real and her mother was overwhelmed with phone calls from parents. Her mother told her she couldn't believe everything she read. Santa **was** real!

"There it is again!"

"What are you talking about?" Tom asked, a little irritated.

"There's something following us further over in the woods!"

"Oh for heaven's sake, will you stop!"

Rhonda was an in-door person. All her interests and activities were carried out inside. Hiking in the woods wasn't exactly her forte. She would have been much happier at home practicing her music or reading a good book or curled up on the couch listening to her favorite concerto.

Tom, on the other hand, was raised on a cattle ranch near Kamloops. His family called him a rough and tumble boy. He loved being outside with his animals and he had plenty of those around. They had the cattle, of course, and horses, and the usual herding dogs. He had his own dog too, a boxer named Mohamed Ali.

He loved walking in the woods on their property and would daydream about the future. He had wonderful, loving parents and his childhood was happy.

When he talked Rhonda into this camping trip, he thought she'd fall in love with the great outdoors the way he did. Now, he was thinking maybe it was a mistake. She kept hearing strange noises and didn't seem to be enjoying herself.

"What in the world made me come on this trip? I knew I would hate it," Rhonda kept thinking. "I think there's a bear after us and I have a phobia of bugs. What am I doing here?"

Rhonda was invited to play in the Okanogan Symphony when she graduated high school and decided to enter the B.C. College of the Interior in Kamloops since the symphony was based there.

Tom entered B.C.C.I. Law School the year Rhonda started her junior year.

They met through mutual friends on the tennis court. It was instant attraction and they made a handsome couple. After their first date, Tom didn't give Rhonda time to date anyone else. He took up all her time. It wasn't as though she minded, but later she wondered if it was wise.

Rhonda talked Tom into coming to the symphony concerts and Tom convinced her she would love camping. He did have some reservations, however, after she told him she was scared to death of anything that "creepeth" or "crawleth."

They had just set up the tent when Rhonda asked, "Where are the restrooms?"

"You're kidding, right?"

"No. Why?"

"Well, I guess the only answer I can give is—find a comfortable log."

"What?"

"I thought you knew. You really aren't the woodsy type, are you," he said with a sneer.

Rhonda relieved herself as seldom as possible that weekend. By the time she got home, she was sure she was going to die from a burst bladder. The next outing, if ever, would have to be at a Provincial Park with facilities. No more "comfortable log" stuff for her!

Tom wanted to get married in this, his final year, but Rhonda wanted to wait until she graduated. However, she was no match for Tom's ardor and they married during Christmas season.

The first *bitter pill* she had to swallow was the day she told Tom she was expecting. It wasn't as though he got angry and he never suggested an abortion. There was no reaction at all, unlike her uncontrollable excitement.

For her, once the news sunk in, she was thrilled and could scarcely believe she had a new human being growing within her. When she saw a picture of the Gerber baby, she welled up with tears.

Tom's reaction hurt and she wondered if she really knew this man she'd married. She was certain that the sarcasm, ridicule and total disinterest in their baby was unlikely to change. The marriage had been a huge mistake.

Today Rhonda finds herself two months pregnant, walking in the woods with her husband who'd hurt her so badly, and some creature was tracking them. She thought, "Not only was Tom lacking in feelings, he apparently can't hear either."

He kept telling her he didn't hear anything and she knew *she* had. He said she was just stupid.

"That's nice! No one has ever called me stupid in my entire life," she thought, biting her tongue to keep from shouting at Tom.

Rhonda certainly did not want to be killed by a bear. Not now! Now that she had a plan for herself and her baby. Deep down inside she knew the plan would not include Tom.

The sound that she'd been hearing all day finally caught Tom's attention. He stopped suddenly and stared into the woods. Rhonda stopped and looked too. Their hearts were pounding and their mouths went dry. Crashing through the underbrush coming straight for them was whatever was making the noises in the woods. Their pounding hearts stopped when the animal broke through the bushes and into the meadow. It was the most beautiful buck either had ever seen. The buck also stopped and stared, then turned on a dime and went back into the woods.

"See, I told you there was nothing to worry about," Tom sneered.

"Get over yourself!" Rhonda replied. "You were as scared as me when you finally heard something. You turned white as a ghost."

As the months went by things didn't change and Rhonda knew she had to put Part I of her Plan in motion or her future would be "this" and nothing more.

"Tom, I'm going to take some classes at night school. I feel as though my brain will atrophy if I don't have some stimulation," Rhonda said as calmly as she could.

"I don't care what you do although I don't understand why you need stimulation."

"Well, it'll also feel good to finish my education and get my degree as I always meant to."

Part I of the plan was going along fine. She felt fortunate that her pregnancy was problem free and didn't interrupt her goal. By the time her due date came, she only had one quarter left to get her teaching degree.

Through the months, she tried to engage Tom in the excitement of bringing a new life into the world. It didn't work. He just wasn't interested in her or the baby. His career was the foremost thing in his life.

When Rhonda went into labor, Tom drove her to the hospital, but when it was evident the labor would be long, he wanted to go home.

"Someone can call me when the baby comes," he told her.

When Rhonda started to cry and after a scornful look from a nurse, he stayed. However, she knew he didn't want to be there.

Nancy Kay Bartlett was born at 5:30 AM the following morning. She was a beautiful, healthy baby and the love Rhonda felt immediately was so overwhelming it surprised even her.

A few weeks after Nancy Kay's birth, it was time for Part II of her Plan. Rhonda found a day care for the baby, finished her last quarter in record time and received her coveted teaching papers.

Every day when Tom left for work, Rhonda sent out resumes to school districts all over the state. She used a P.O. Box as the return address unbeknownst to Tom.

She received a few replies and made an appointment for her first interview. It was at an elementary school in a small town about fifty miles north of their home in San Francisco.

The interview went very well. She liked the area, the school, and the principal. Two weeks later Rhonda was offered the job and readily accepted.

Part III of the plan was at hand and the Plan could be completed.

The next day she went to the bank and withdrew 2/3 of their monies, packed all she could of her and Nancy's belongings into the SUV. She took out the letter for Tom she had been composing for months. She sealed it and put it on the mantle.

She buckled the baby into her car seat and backed out of the driveway.

After she pulled onto the freeway, she glanced at her daughter and said, "Okay, Nancy Kay! We're going on an adventure to a new life. Just you and me!"

The Plan is complete.

Some of My Poems

Beyond

Along the edge of the field,
Past the edge of the city, he walked

On the highway between the two towns,
Into this darkest deep path, he walked

Behind the eerily glowing cottage,
Down the trail towards the river, he walked

Into the river beneath the bridge,
Beneath the wonderfully warm waterfall, he walked

Toward the deafening sound like thunder,
Beyond everything but the clouds
And he was gone

The Man on the Street

Be kinder than need be, to all that you meet
A smile and hello is a good way to greet

The battle he fights, you may not know
He has his pride, but won't let it show

The problems he has could be your own
He lives on the street and feels all alone

It's not easy for him to live day by day
Plans snuffed out, that's always the way

The rule is, "Don't judge a book by its cover."
Prior to now, he wouldn't look like this! Ever!

Through no fault of his own, he finds himself here
With no one willing to lend him an ear

It is hard to remember the life he once had
He wonders how things got so bad

The smile you give him, at no cost to you
Could possibly change his view

So, be kinder than need be, to all that you meet
A smile and hello is a good way to greet

Choices

Life's been a challenge
If the truth were to tell
Being alone,
Is my glimpse of hell

Such is my lot
I have born it well
There is still laughter and
An occasional rebel yell

They say we should be wary
Of the choices we make
I tried, but circumstance and duty
My choices, they take

I chose to capture
Contentment for my sake
I'm left with, right or wrong,
Remembrance in the wake

Poor Little Heart

Sometimes I consider my heart
Separate from me
It seems to hurt less that way

I set it aside and
Do my best
To carry on

We all have times in our lives
Which seem too hard to bear
There's a break in us that occurs

This break is painful
Out of our control
It takes time to mend

Time seems to stop
It seems an eternity
While waiting to heal

Because of you, my friends
And with the help of God
My poor broken heart
Will come back to me—whole

My Credo

I believe in the Fatherhood
And communion of God our creator

The Leadership and Spirit of Jesus;
The goodness in mankind

The freedom to reason
The pursuit of truth and the love of God

My Truth

I listened and studied through all of my years
I found one can't believe each word that one hears
I know I can question without any fear

I am content with what I deem right
This is truth, solely in *my* sight
Still I feel God has shown me His light

Alpha & Omega

Beginning

Love
Hope
Purpose

End

Disappointment
Love lost
Hope gone
Burning anger
Throbbing pain

Beginning

Love
Hope
Purpose

End

Completion
Love everlasting
Hope abounding
Restful calm
Contentment

The choice is yours!

Previously published in the Senior Scene Newspaper

Karen's Stories

Karen Saxon

Karen Saxon resides in Puyallup, Washington with her husband of forty-five years. Karen has always written, mostly for her own pleasure, either poetry or essays. In her job for the Puyallup School District she wrote a column for the Science Newsletter.

In retirement she promised herself to pursue a writing class and perfect those long dormant skills. Karen credits the Puyallup Writer's Workshop, a critique group at the Puyallup Activity Center, for challenging her to write fiction, composing at the computer and honing those writing techniques.

Karen is currently working on a cooking memoir for her family.

Happy Birthday to Me

Ten Minute Writing Exercise

By
Karen Saxon

It is a warm sunny day in the late spring. Cherry blossoms have faded and the trees are beginning to set fruit. Apple blossoms fill the air with their sweet pink fragrance and I inhale the smell of the freshly mown orchard grass. It's a clean, just washed smell like sheets on the clothesline.

It's a picnic! I shall celebrate my eleventh birthday with a few school friends and my sisters. The table is spread and a picnic basket awaits opening for good eats and birthday treats.

The table is special. Dad fashioned it from an old hay wagon that had been left on the farm we now own. No longer useful for hauling hay it supports 2 x 6 planks from fore to aft axle, for seating. The wheels make a decorative statement as it sets in the orchard. I love having my birthday here. It's like a private place, quiet except for birds heralding warmer weather, the bees pollinating the trees and an errant mosquito now and then adding its tune.

Yes, Happy Birthday to me! It's a good day, friends, family and hotdogs on a stick in the fire pit!

Starlight Birthday Cake

Sift together:
2 cups and 2 tablespoons all purpose flour
3 teaspoons baking powder
1 ½ sugar
1 teaspoon salt
Add:
½ c. shortening
1 cup milk
1 teaspoon vanilla or other flavoring
Beat two minutes and add two medium eggs.
Beat two minutes more
Pour into two greased and floured eight inch cake rounds.
Bake @ 350 degrees for thirty to thirty five minutes.

Remove from pans, cool completely and frost with:

Beat 'N' Eat Frosting

1 egg white, room temperature, unbeaten
¾ cup sugar
¼ teaspoon cream of tartar
1 teaspoon vanilla

Mix well in deep bowl.
Slowly add ¼ cup of boiling water.
Beat with mixer until stiff peaks form.

Melt half a package of semi-sweet chocolates chips (or equivalent in bar chocolate) in bowl over simmering water.

Frost first layer of cake for filling and spoon chocolate over the frosting.

Add top layer and frost top and sides with meringue icing.

With the back of a spoon dip the chocolate and make swirls in the meringue icing.

Let set to dry.

Yum!

Excerpt from Memories and Munchings, Recipes from Life

Loretta's Stories

Loretta Hagen Walker

Loretta grew up on the Hagen sheep ranch in North Central Idaho at White Bird, Idaho. She was an only daughter with three brothers and her formative years were spent helping her Mother with gardening and cooking. After attending the University of Idaho for a year, she married her high school boy friend and they eventually settled in Pullman Washington in 1962 and raised five children.

In Pullman she shared food and baked items with neighbors and eventually created a catering business serving the needs of the community and WSU until 1982 when she entered WSU as an undergraduate and graduated with a degree in nutrition in 1986.

Eventually life changed and she moved to Tacoma and worked as a clinical dietitian for nine years and retired. Loretta likes to write stories of the ranch years, gardening, canning and cooking are her passions.

Loretta plans to move from Tacoma to Washtucna, Washington with her partner Robert this fall. There she will write, garden, can, travel and help her daughter and family in their business.

Chocolates on a Winter Day

By
Loretta Walker

In this 1920's snapshot, Myrtie, my mother, sits astride a saddle horse on a mountain ridge near White Bird, Idaho. She's bundled warm in a wool coat and a wool hat is jauntily pulled to one side on her stylish twenties bobbed hair. A leather-gloved left hand holds a candy box, lined with white paper, while slim bare fingers of the right hand, tease her lips with a chocolate. Perhaps it's Valentine's Day or November 16, her birthday.

While perched there on the face of the earth, no matter what cold winter day it is, her heart must be warmed by the gift. Her deep-set brown eyes look toward the giver of the chocolates in a coquettish manner, suggestive of a warm reward to the one who gives this gift-of-the-gods on a special day.

Myrtie (Mom) learned in her formative years the taste of chocolate candy. In the winter of 1916, still a teen-ager at home, she prepared fudge on a wood cook stove. This kind of sweet reward food preparation surely helped create a passion for chocolates as well as her lifetime pleasure of preparing and serving homemade desserts to our family.

January 27, 1916 at fifteen, she writes in her diary:

> *This evening I made fudge. It fell flat. I put it in so the chocolate curdled the milk. It said to cook it until it formed a ball in soft water. And the plagued stuff wouldn't ball. I cooked & I cooked & I cooked. I got it lots too hard but it was good just the same.*

Less than a month later, a teenager soothes her desperate burgeoning chocoholic sweet tooth tendencies by whipping up a batch of fudge before going to church.

February 12, 1916 she wrote:

> *I had to go to the church at 7:30 to a Sunday school doings. At six I started in to make fudge and it wouldn't fudge. I cooked it three or four times and at last got it too hard, but it was mighty good, believe me.*

In those days, for a teenager, cooking on top of the wood stove was easier than tempering the oven for baking. Making fudge was a one-pan procedure so there were not many dishes to wash by hand. Grandpa had a milk cow, therefore butter, milk and cream was always plentiful. As well as stored sugar and cocoa in the cupboard available. Deciding what to cook from scratch was easy.

Dad must have remembered the rewards of candy, because he bought chocolate for Mom on Mother's Day and birthdays. Sometimes to surprise her, usually with boxes of Whitman Samplers, the chocolate choice in Idaho County. I remember, when she opened the box to share, our mouths watered and fingers itched to reach for one as we tried to remember which chocolate squiggle designated the dark chocolate one with nuts, the favorite of everyone. We could have one, or maybe two pieces, and then Mom put the box away in the linen closet in her bedroom to be taken out again at her whim, to share her chocolates.

Many old candy boxes of the nineteen-thirty's and forty's were wooden with lovely pictures on the lids. I treasure the one I have with two winged gold lions guarding a naked lady whose loins are covered by a gold leafed branch. It's covered with a faux leather padded paper on the top with bright pink taffeta lining the inside and a mirror on the hinged lid. Though worn, it's nice enough to display some of Mom's old jewelry inside.

We had an extensive orchard and though fruit desserts and canned fruit were our everyday meal choice, a tin of Hershey's cocoa and a box of Bakers unsweetened chocolate resided under the kitchen counter to be used for those predictable chocolate cravings. We made from scratch; puddings, chocolate cakes, cupcakes, cookies, cocoa and fudge. We rarely made brownies or chocolate chip cookies. They were not the rage then and perhaps chocolate chips weren't so available as well as the extra cost. When we did use chocolate chips, it would be to add a handful to oatmeal cookies as I do today.

My brother Richard saved a letter I wrote to him when he was at the University of Idaho, indicating I was baking and helping in the kitchen at ten years of age.

October 3, 1947:

> *I made some cookies today made them with cocoa. I just put some in the oven. Well, I have to set the table.*

Fudge making on a cold winter night on the kitchen wood stove that also heated one half of the house was a normal activity especially when my friends from the neighboring ranch, Pat and Charlene Bentz, came to stay overnight. We made fudge from scratch, that is without marshmallow cream and chocolate chips for fun. If there was more than one person it was added muscle power to stir until it was thick and glossy. After pouring it into a buttered square pan, we argued over who licked the spoon or scraped the pan clean. We impatiently waited at least fifteen minutes for the first cut or spoon of fudge, depending on our success cooking it.

My brothers also made fudge. They had the muscle power and Mother never said no. Richard, my oldest brother made fudge as a teen in the early forties before he joined the Army. His favorite recipe exists in Mother's old patched together recipe book, or perhaps it was hers from her teen years when she made fudge for fun.

Richard's Fudge:

2/3 Cup Cocoa	1 ½ Tablespoon Corn Syrup
3 Cups Sugar	1 1/2 Cup Milk
1/8 Tsp. Salt	¾ Tsp Vanilla
4 ½ Tablespoon Butter	

Combine and bring to boil, stirring often, cocoa, sugar, salt, syrup and milk.
Bring to soft boil stage, remove from heat and add butter.
Beat until glossy and pour into buttered pan. Cool and cut into squares.

What is so special about chocolate? It's tasty, hard to resist and makes a great gift and it is touted as healthy and good for you. With so many chocolate companies, it has become a common everyday food and one can stand around and compare tastes and brag that you eat this brand or that brand, and justify that it's healthy and then continue to indulge.

I think it's better to hide chocolates including those bowls of M & M's and Hershey's Kisses in the linen closet. Only bring them out when the keeper of the chocolates considers someone is worthy to share them, or open a box of chocolates on a winter day given by your admirer while sitting on a saddle horse, high on a ridge in Idaho County near White Bird. That would be an experience to brag about.

Some of my favorite chocolate recipes

Chocolate Applesauce Cake

2 cups flour
½ cup Dutch-process cocoa powder
1 teaspoon baking soda and ½ teaspoon salt
Sift together dry ingredients.

2 cups applesauce
(if homemade applesauce is very thick,
thin with a little water before measuring)
1 ½ cups sugar
½ cup oil I use canola or light olive oil
2 eggs
2 teaspoons vanilla extract
½ cup chopped walnuts
(or as much as you like, but hard to cut if too many)
½ cup semisweet miniature chocolate chips

Preheat oven to 350 degrees.

Sift together flour, cocoa, baking soda and salt into large bowl.

Mix in large mixer bowl, together applesauce, sugar, oil, eggs and vanilla until blended. Add dry ingredients and mix well. Scrape up bottom of bowl.

Spread batter into greased 13x9-inch pan and smooth top. Or divide into two equal size smaller pans. Sprinkle evenly with walnuts and chocolate chips.

Bake until toothpick inserted in center comes out clean,

30 to 35 minutes or less for smaller pans.

Keep checking with toothpick and take out of oven just when dry.

Let cool at least 15 minutes before cutting and serving.

HOT FUDGE SAUCE

30 large marshmallows (about ½ large bag)
2/3 cup milk
¼ cup butter
Dash salt
1 (12 o z) package semi-sweet chocolate chips

1 ½ teaspoons vanilla

Put marshmallows, milk, butter and salt into a heavy saucepan over low heat; stir frequently until melted and blended. Remove from heat.

Add chocolate chips and vanilla all at once and stir until all the chips are melted.

Serve warm over ice cream. Store in fridge.

For gifts, pour the hot sauce into hot, sterilized jars, let cool, then put lids on jars and refrigerate.

Before serving, the sauce may be quickly warmed in the microwave oven.

Yields 2 cups

Adapted from San Francisco Chronicle Oct. 2005

Hot Fudge Pudding

1 cup sifted flour
2 tsp. baking powder ¼ tsp. salt
¾ cup sugar 2 tbsp. cocoa

Stir in . . . ½ cup milk and 2 tbsp. oil

Blend in . . . 1 cup chopped nuts
Spread in 9 inch square pan.
Sprinkle with mixture of
1 cup brown sugar (packed)
¼ cup cocoa
Pour 1 ¾ cups hot water over entire batter . . .

Bake 350 degrees about 45 minutes.
During baking, cake mixture rises to top and

chocolate sauce settles to bottom.
Invert squares of pudding on dessert plates.
Serve warm, with or without whipped cream.

Adapted from Betty Crocker Cookbook from 50s

Mother and I and Watermelons

By
Loretta Hagen Walker

My birthday celebration dinner always included a home grown watermelon, usually the first one of the season. Mother prepared a harvest dinner of fried chicken and fresh vegetables from the garden followed by cake, homemade ice cream and watermelon. The usual crew gathered for dinner, the same that sat down three times a day to our dinning room table: Dad, brothers Lars and Steve, maybe Richard, Grandpa Hagen, three or four hired men and Mom and I. A fryer chicken or two was selected from the flock that ran free in the grassy back yard: a handy proximity to grab them, hold their head to a chopping block and later prepared for frying. Along with the fine fryer, we were served potatoes and gravy, corn on the cob, sliced red ripe tomatoes, rounds of sweet cucumbers and onions marinated in cider vinegar with a sprinkle of pepper and salt. This harvest meal also included fresh-homemade rolls, churned sweet butter and strawberry jam canned earlier in the summer from our berries. It was my birthday and dessert included the anticipated first of the season, red ripe watermelon.

I was destined to become Mother's helper and worked by her side even in the garden. Watermelons became my specialty. Thus, I claimed the watermelon patch as my domain and my melons. In the hot summer, by the age of four or five years, as instructed by Mother, I learned that melons require a lot of garden space and plenty of water supplied by little irrigation ditches.

In late May seeds gathered and saved from last years crop were planted in little mounds of soil about five feet apart. Plants emerged from the warm soil and grew to masses of green foliage on spreading vines. Blossoms came next, tucked among the leaves of the sprawling plants. Bees hummed as they flitted from flower to flower, their little feet pollinating, assuring babies to the parent plant. Then light green watermelons emerged at the blossom end. I might count half a dozen melons forming on one plant. I respected the fragile baby melons forming under a blanket of vine and did not touch them. Eventually like growing teenagers bursting the buttons on their jeans, the green melons revealed themselves in the sprawling vines. The earliest set blossoms yielded the first fruit. Eventually, I discovered fast developing melons and watch them grow larger over the summer. Picking the best watermelon in the patch was like a treasure hunt. Through out the summer, I'd hoed and irrigated, thus gained the privilege to pick the one with which to celebrate my birthday.

A couple of weeks before my birthday, brother Steve joined me to test the watermelons; finger plunking them frequently to determine which melon was near its prime. To plunk a melon we held the first or second finger by the thumb then released smack against the fruit, listening for the watermelon's voice, a dull thud which would indicate a fully ripe watermelon. Its main ingredient, water, with natural sugar, would have caused the melon to swell to twenty-plus pounds. Its sound changed as the melon ripened and over the years of finger plunking watermelons, especially from age three, one recognized the voice of a ripe melon. Also as the watermelons grew fatter and elongated, the bright green color became dull. Nearing the picking stage we checked for other indicators of ripeness by turning the melon over to look for the field spot or yellowing of the underside. We checked the drying tendril and two little leaves where the vine attached to the melon like an umbilical chord.

When I was young, early in the morning before the sun heated the melons, Mother and I would select and pick one. Still cool, it would remain on the back porch until time to cut open. Frequently my brothers and I lacked self discipline to wait until it was cut and served on a platter in the dining room. Thus we plugged it by cutting a small triangle into the melon with a paring knife, then tip the knife to force the piece out, just enough for a bite. The rind was replaced. We knew right away if we had a good one. A fresh field melon's delightful essence was released to our nose while just one glance and taste determined if our learned knowledge as well as intuition was accurate.

Then we would have to wait until dinner. When a large sharp knife blade was stabbed into the watermelon, it should ring with an audible crack or splitting sound and you knew you hit the jackpot when it exploded with fragrance and super saturated sweetness.

One summer a few watermelons, still in the ripening stage, were beginning to spoil in the garden on the ground. Mother blamed Steve, who was about eight years old for plugging watermelons in the patch. She had to eat crow when a hired man chomped down on some bird shot in a piece of melon at dinner. My older brother Lars had been shooting the 4-10 shot gun at red-winged black birds pecking at corn planted near the watermelons.

After dark, another time, we heard the dogs barking and out the window saw a flashlight moving and bobbing about in the garden. The light headed toward the watermelon patch. Brave brother Lars went to investigate. He never came back to the house to report on the trespassers. Lars obviously turned thief and helped his friends raid my watermelon patch! I knew then there had been collusion with those rascals.

Today watermelons aren't what they were then. The fruit, sold in the produce department of big grocery stores year around, the protective rind pared away and cut in squares, resides in plastic trays like a shrinking mass of sticky pink cotton candy. Pry open the plastic lid and it lacks sweetness, fragrance or flavor. Even if purchased whole, they are what they are-old melons.

Advertised by the grocers, the watermelon season gets its kick off for the annual $4^{th\ of}$ July barbecue. The actual melon season is still a few weeks away. A watermelon shipped from thousands of miles away is like a 4th of July sparkler without the sparkle, a dud.

A summer watermelon planted in their regional hot climates when sliced, provides a pleasurable bonus of hydration as cells of the fruit explode with sugar-water sweetness quenching thirst, delighting the senses. Watermelons need to be field ripened and then picked, cooled, split open and eaten within a few hundred yards of where they're grown. Without that experience the general public just doesn't know how to choose one at the store or what real watermelon tastes like.

In my mind, one could never choose a good watermelon unless when very young at your Mother side, you tended to its growth in the garden.

1919: Myrtie, my Mother on the right, dressed in a summer white dress, eating watermelon, her favorite home grown treat.

Peaches and Cream

By
Loretta Hagen Walker

I crave fresh sweet peaches in the summer. Do you dare to eat a peach, a delicious fruit tree ripened in its healthy green environment? Within reach or on a ladder you may extend your arm and gently twist one free that clings to a sturdy limb. I admire the fruit, marvel at its cream-colored fuzzy coat that protects the blush of skin covering its juicy flesh.

One bite, a burst of sweet succulent juice may escape through your lips down your chin, dropping onto your breast. Picked fresh off a tree, it takes courage to eat this juicy summer fruit.

T. S. Eliot's poem, *The Love Song of J Alfred Prufrock* is a favorite because of this line; "Do I dare to eat a peach?" In the heat of summer, eating a whole fresh peach, dripping with fragrant juice, takes courage. Prufrock didn't have it. He would be embarrassed. Age gripped him; life had passed. He worried peach juice would stain his creased white pants.

Not so with Sarah in Shelby Hearon's book, *Life Estates*. Sarah falls for the allure of her peaches. On the first page of the book, Sarah who lives in Georgia looks out the window as she talks on the phone and silently admires her tree fruit, the Georgia Belle, the Monroe, the Tyler, and the O'Henry, "as dear to me as kin." Later, Sarah purposely makes three peach desserts for a dinner party with three different types of peaches. She mentions to her guests, "I could smell the different peach essence as the steam from the cobbler and pie mingled with the cold fresh peach aroma of the shortcake slices." She wonders to herself if someone else had made the three desserts, could she identify which peach was in which dish.

As a young girl, I helped mother pick peaches from our small ranch orchard. We had two large trees. A Red Haven was delicious for fresh eating and an heirloom Alberta that was firm and good for canning, although we did preserve both varieties.

Canning was hard work in the daily ninety to one hundred degree hot summers in White Bird, Idaho. There were many steps in preparation to preserve the fruit: Pick the peaches. Wash and rinse quart jars with hot water by hand. Make simple syrup in a kettle with one part sugar to two parts water or to taste with less sugar. Bring syrup to boil. To loosen the skin, scald the peaches with boiling water, immediately plunge into cold water to stop them from cooking. Gently peel the peaches. The loose skins slip off easily, cut in half, discard pit and place fruit in the clean jars. Pour the syrup over the peaches. Seal with jar lids and rings and place seven quarts in a canner and cover with water. Bring to a rolling boil on the hot wood stove in the kitchen and gently boil for twenty minutes. Carefully remove the hot jars from the canner and repeat the process. Mother and I canned fifty to one hundred quarts of peaches every summer.

We prepared and served fresh desserts and made peach preserves too. Our family appreciated the taste and aroma of summer captured in jars by our own hands. As a young girl, a pre-teen in this twenty first century language, I thought it all a delightful experience from the eating to the canning as well as the lovely sight of our jars of fruit stored in the pantry. These jars were lined on shelves and admired as one walked by, easy to grab one and open for a delicious quick supper dessert.

Year after year this peachy summer delicacy was enjoyed by family and hired men. In the spring, we delighted in the promising swirl of pink blossoms in the orchard to later serving peeled sliced peaches lightly dusted with sugar for dinner dessert. Adding to this delicious sparkle, we served sweet cream, which early in the morning, was separated from whole milk.

Later in my professional role in life, I went to a food and wine conference and heard a nationally known writer and farmer David mas Masumoto speak with passion about his peach orchard in California and his quest to save his fragile but best tasting peaches. I bought his book,

Epitaph for a Peach. Later I read he would give a reading at the Tacoma Public library to promote a new book, *Four Seasons in a Year,* which I couldn't resist buying.

Enhanced by stories from books and my peachy lifetime experiences, this exceptional summer treat becomes a delicacy. Not a cardboard tasting hard fruit from the grocery store but a juicy, sweet peach of summer. Picked ripe from a tree in the back yard with just one bite, the juices will drip. You'd best lean over the sink or have a cloth handy to wipe the sweet juice your tongue can't reach.

As I walk by the shelves in my pantry, I admire the summer canning; the fruits of my labor. The golden peaches radiate like a sunrise through the glass and I react by reaching for a small jar of peach preserves. Perhaps I should make a pan of biscuits to accompany the syrupy fruit slices. But if I do, will I dare to stop eating all of it at once? I doubt it.

Peach Preserves

6 lb. Net. Wt. peeled and sliced peaches
4 lb. sugar
1 pouch liquid pectin, if necessary

Alternately, layer the peaches and the sugar, beginning with fruit and ending with sugar. Cover and refrigerate for 24 hours or up to 3 days. Strain fruit. Boil syrup over med. Heat until it reaches 230 degrees, about 30 min. Add drained fruit to the hot syrup and cook until mixture is 217 degrees. Ladle into sterilized jars. Cover with lids and rings. Process in hot water bath for 5 minutes.

Peach & Berry Cobbler

Filling
3 lb peaches, peeled and sliced into ½ inch slices
1 pt fresh blueberries,
1 pint black berries, 1 ½ tbsp. cornstarch
1/4 tsp nutmeg and ½ cup sugar

Topping
2 cups flour
½ cup sugar
½ tsp. soda
½ tsp baking powder
¼ tsp salt
1 stick cold butter
7 oz pkg almond paste
1 cup buttermilk

375-degree oven

Grease 13 x 9 baking dish

Stir together sugar, cornstarch and nutmeg. Toss/or stir into fruit.

Pour into baking dish. Bake for 10 min. while preparing almond topping.

Sift flour, sugar, soda, baking powder and salt into a medium bowl.

On the large-hole side of a box grater, grate the butter and almond paste into flour mixture. Mix with fingers until the dough is the texture of small crumbs (or use a food processor, or pastry cutter). Add buttermilk, and stir until just mixed. Don't over mix.

Remove baking dish from oven, and drop dough by rounded tablespoons on top of hot fruit. Return dish to oven and bake for 35 minutes more, or until fruit is bubbly and biscuit topping is golden brown.

Easy Peach Cobbler

Preheat oven to 375 degrees
½ cube butter
4-6 cups fruit, peaches, or a combination of fruit
1 cup flour
1 cup sugar
½ tsp. salt
2 tsp. baking powder
1 cup milk

Toss peeled fruit, cut in slices, in ¾ cup sugar.
Heat up to boiling in microwave or on stovetop.

Melt butter in 13 x 9 baking dish.
Combine rest of ingredients.
Pour batter over hot butter in baking dish.
Spoon fruit on top of batter
Bake for 30 to 45 minutes

This is an old recipe from the 1950's. We used a jar of canned peaches.

The Temptation of Red Apples

By
Loretta Hagen Walker

I remember it was a typical White Bird, Idaho, scorching hot summer day in 1944. Mom, Grandma Hagen, my little brother Steve and I were picking apples from a tree that stood tall by the garden path north of Grandma's house. My assigned job was to pick up the fallen apples on the ground. I wanted to climb on the ladder to pick, but they always thought young kids especially this young girl should never be allowed that adult privilege. Sometimes, Steve has to climb because, even though he is younger, he's a boy.

I thought, adults tell little kids to do jobs like picking up apples in the nasty weeds because they don't want to bend over to do it. I pouted as I resigned myself to this chore, wondering why I had to be out here on this hot, sticky day with the tall-stemmed bushy blooms of the pigweed, scratching my bare legs and arms.

The sun blazed and warm apples sent a fragrant spicy aroma to my nose. Thoughts of Mom's cinnamon applesauce for supper perked my spirits. I knew after we were home she'd prepare and cook the fallen apples. She would sit and rest, balancing a pan of apples in her lap to peel, core and cut out any spots or brown bruises with a paring knife. She'd slice the apples, add a little sugar, dash of cinnamon and a splash of water, then cook on the stove to make the sauce. Maybe she would make gingerbread. Suddenly cooperating with the adults seemed bearable.

Low in a ditch, I spied a large red apple peeking through the weeds. Oh, what a nice one I thought. I moved toward it and stopped. As I gazed at the apple, I felt my skin burned from the sun and the weeds scratched my bare legs. I wanted to go back to the comfort of Grandma's cool house.

Grasshoppers jumped as mom stepped through the weeds. "There's a big apple over there in the ditch," Mom said. I stood quiet, staring at the red apple, mesmerized by what I saw.

Mom spoke louder, "Sister, go pick up the apple."

"I don't want to. There's a snake over there." I whispered.

Hidden in the weeds coiled against the red apple like a cat lying snug ready to pounce on a mouse, was a rattler.

Grandma and Mom grabbed the buckets and Steve and I happily followed onto the path. We all headed lickety-split, to the safety of the Grandma's house.

Lovely apples nestled in weeds are temping but might be dangerous for little girls. Is this where the saying *a snake in the grass* came from? Little girls, beware . . .

XXX

Applesauce

I like homemade applesauce but not the pureed, strained type. Real applesauce that remains identifiable as made from real apples. I peel, slice, and add a little water, dash of lemon juice and sugar to taste. After the apples are cooked to a desirable sauce, I add a sprinkle of cinnamon on top. One does not need a recipe to make applesauce but I have made this Martha Stewart recipe and it is good.

Spicy Applesauce

6 pounds cooking apples (about 18) peeled, cored, and quartered
1 cup apple cider
1 cinnamon stick
½ vanilla bean
½ teaspoon nutmeg
½ teaspoon mace
Juice of one lemon (about 2 tablespoons)

Combine apples, apple cider, spices and lemon juice in a large wide heavy saucepan. Cook stirring often to prevent scorching until the apples are cooked. Takes up to 1 hour.

Remove from heat and let stand to cool completely.

Remove cinnamon stick and vanilla bean.

Albert's Stories

Albert E. Farrar Jr.

Al credits his first writing piece to a sixth grade assignment given by his teacher, but it wasn't until 2005 that he began to write seriously. He took a class and from that came short stories and a three book series, which has been published.

The first book was called, THE WORLD OF JACK DENNISON—DETECTIVE. The same title is used in all three books of the series distinguished only by (A CONTINUING STORY) and (THE FINAL CHAPTER) on books two and three.

Al feels he has been fortunate in having talented people assist him in getting his books together.

He is also hopeful to be able to publish a book of short stories in the near future. It will be a variety of stories, much different from his three book series. It is an effort currently in progress.

When not writing, Al and his wife travel, visit family and friends and stay as active as possible.

The Kids

By
Albert E. Farrar Jr.

The kids were playing hide and seek outside grandmother's house in the woods. When dinner was ready all the children came running but one.

"Where's Jimmy?" grandma asked after she looked around and did not see him at the table.

"I don't know," replied Jacob. "Maybe he didn't hear you call."

"We were playing Hide and Seek. Maybe he's still hiding," said Mary.

"Okay," Grandma said. "You all go and look for him. I'll keep everything warm. Come back in five minutes. Don't go too far," she called after them.

They all headed for the door, across the porch and into the huge back yard with the woods several hundred yards beyond Grandma's house.

"Jimmy. Jimmy." Grandma could hear them all calling as they headed out across the yard in all directions. Into the woods several of them ventured. Behind and into the barn went two others. Soon they too were also out of sight. Several minutes passed and finally they all started to return, one by one.

"I can't find him," said Mary. "He didn't answer."

So it was with them all. Grandma had them all sit down, and as she fed them, she wondered where that little rascal Jimmy went. He wouldn't miss dinner. She was sure of that. Of all the kids in her charge, Jimmy was the one who was always hungry.

Meanwhile deep in the woods a young boy named Jimmy was marveling at all the things he was seeing for the first time. He'd never gone this deep before. The trees were everywhere and they were so tall. He couldn't even see the light from the sky any more.

Suddenly, walking around an especially large tree, he saw something very unusual. It was a path and Jimmy being inquisitive, started to follow it. Soon the foliage covered the entire path and he could no longer see the other trees in the forest. On he went and then around a bend in the path, he saw stairs going down into the ground.

Jimmy looked around and seeing nothing but vines covering the path he'd been walking on, he looked down the steps. He could not see where they were going, but being a curious young lad, Jimmy started to walk down the stairs. First one, then two and three and on he went. It was a very long stair case.

Finally Jimmy came to the bottom and straight ahead just a few feet beyond, was a big door. It was the largest door he'd ever seen. As he walked closer, it started to open.

Jimmy walked through the opening and into a very large room. It was beautiful with huge columns going straight up into the sky. Off to his left he could see some people. They were very little. They were even smaller than he was. They were all busy working at something, but he didn't know what it was. To his right, he noticed some other tiny people fixing food. They were busy scurrying back and forth as fast as they could and it looked like they could not get things done fast enough.

As he was looking at all these things going on around him, a tiny voice spoke out.

"Hello Jimmy."

He looked down to his left and there was the smallest person he'd ever seen. Jimmy wasn't very big since he was only seven years old, and this person only came up to his knee.

"Hello. Who are you?" Jimmy asked.

"I'm Mosee," the little person said.

"Where am I?" Jimmy asked.

"You are in fanciful land."

"Fanciful land? What's that?"

"It's a place where you can imagine whatever you want." said Mosee

"Really?" asked Jimmy.

"Yes. Anything you want."

"Wow! You mean I can imagine that I'm an astronaut in space?"

"That's right."

"How do I do that?" asked a very anxious Jimmy.

"Just close your eyes and say out loud, *I am an astronaut in space.* Then open your eyes and look around and there you are."

Jimmy closed his eyes tightly and said in a loud voice, "I am an astronaut in space."

He opened his eyes and looked around. There he was. There were three other astronauts in their space suits busy working on different things. Jimmy looked down at his clothes and he too was dressed in a space suit.

Suddenly a voice called his name.

"Jimmy," said the voice. "What's the reading on your big dial?'

Jimmy looked at the big dial in front of him, not quite sure what it was. It read 139.24.

"Hurry up" the voice said."

"139.24," Jimmy replied.

"Okay thanks," the voice said.

Jimmy continued to look around when one of the other Astronauts asked.

"What's the reading on the outside temperature gauge now?"

Jimmy looked around trying to find where the gauge was. It seemed all so complicated. But there it was. Just down and to the right of the big one he'd just read.

"It reads Minus 129.2337," Jimmy called out.

"Thanks Jimmy," said the voice

He looked around the small space capsule at all the instruments wondering what they all were.

Suddenly the first astronaut spoke again. "Okay let's get ready to re-enter earth's atmosphere. Everything set Jimmy?" the voice asked.

Jimmy was scared. He didn't know what to do. He didn't know if every thing was set.

"Jimmy," the voice called. "Jimmy"

"What?" Jimmy replied.

"How was your space trip?" The voice said.

Jimmy looked around. It was Mosee.

"Oh! Oh! It was great. It was so real. Can I do something else?"

"Not now," Mosee said. "I can hear your grandmother calling. It's dinner time."

"Oh!" Jimmy said. "I guess I'd better go. Grandma gets very upset if I'm late. "Can I come again?"

"Sure," said Mosee. "Just follow the trail to the stairs."

"Bye," called Jimmy as he watched the big door close behind him. He ran up the stairs and back into the forest. When he reached the top step Jimmy started running so Grandma wouldn't be too mad at him being late. Then all of a sudden he stopped and looked around on the ground.

"I'd better mark this spot so I can find it next time. I want to go back on another space ride. He reached down to pick up a few rocks to mark the trail and when he turned around once more to mark the path, it was gone. There was no path.

All Jimmy could see was the forest around him and the sky above. There was no path and there wasn't anything other than the trees and bushes found in other parts of the forest.

"Oh, come on Jimmy. What kind of story is that? Asked Billy. Stairs leading into the ground and a big door.

"And little people?" questioned Mary.

"It's just another of those big stories he's always telling," said Joey.

"Now children. Leave Jimmy alone," said Grandma.

A Body At The Foot Of The Stairs

By
Albert E. Farrar Jr.

Maria finished putting on the last of her make-up, turned and walked back into the bedroom she'd left a bit earlier. Neatly placed next to her bed were the shoes she would wear that day. As she sat on the bed, she slipped her nylon covered feet into the inexpensive black shoes with their two inch heels. She hated wearing them. They hurt her feet, but the job required her to look like the executive she was trying to be. Picking up her jacket that matched the skirt she was wearing that day, she slipped her arm into the left sleeve and walked into the living room of her small apartment while she finished putting it on the rest of the way. Stopping near the end table, she picked up her purse, slipped the strap over her shoulder and headed toward the door. She stopped partway and murmured.

"I'd better not forget my cell phone in case Dexter calls. He never calls on the office phone and I don't want to miss anything he might have planned for us. She went through her apartment door and turned toward the stairs of her second floor apartment.

Maria stopped and reached back to check and make sure her door was locked. She'd learned many years ago as a young girl to always check when leaving. It was locked.

Quickly she headed down the stairs to catch her bus. Suddenly, halfway down at the landing, she stopped. There at the bottom of the stairs lay a body. It was a man, she was sure, and he wasn't moving. Maria stood frozen several steps above where the body lay motionless.

Startled at finding this situation, and unsure what to do, she looked around.

First down the hall on the level below her; then back up the stairs and finally down at the body and then at the front door. Just then in through the front door burst a police officer followed by her neighbor, Jim Anders, who lived at the end of the hall on her floor. She'd talked to Jim Anders a few times in passing, but never really got to know him. He'd moved in only a couple of months earlier. The Police Officer glanced up at her and then down at the body on the floor. He examined it briefly and then on his

Radio/phone called for an investigation team.

"Can I get by?" she asked. "I need to get to work."

"You'd better stay here Miss," the officer responded. "The detectives will want to talk to everyone in the building. "But I have to go to work," she implored.

"Better call and tell them you'll be late," he replied. Maria turned back up the stairs and Jim Anders moving around the body followed her. At the top of the stairs, Maria stopped in front of her apartment door.

Ms. Phillips," he said attracting her attention. She turned toward him.

"I've never had an opportunity to talk to you or meet you before, but I'm Jim Anders." "Yes, I know," she replied.

"You do?" he questioned a bit surprised.

"Yes, Agnes Benson told me your name when you moved in."

He chuckled, "Yes. I guess she knows everyone. She quizzed me right away and wanted to know who I was, where I came from, how long I was staying, if I was married and a lot of other things. She even told me about you and that you were single."

Maria laughed in a gentle way knowing exactly how Agnes Benson was. She was a lovely elderly lady, who lived on the first floor, but a lady who always felt a need to know everything about everyone. Maria remembered that Agnes Benson was always asking her if she'd met a young man yet. She must have felt it was her duty to check. She wasn't going to be satisfied until all single people found someone to be with. Maria was sure of that.

"Since we can't leave yet," Jim Anders said, "Would you care to join me for a cup of coffee? I usually grab a cup at the corner coffee shop, but today," he hesitated, "today I couldn't.

Maria paused a moment. She had to call work and tell them she'd be late, and when she'd done that, well there wasn't anything else to do until the detectives arrived. "Sure, why not?" she replied.

"Good. I'll get some started," he said as he moved a step toward his apartment at the end of the hall. Then stopping he turned toward her and said. "I'm sorry. Maybe you'd rather not come to my apartment since we only just met."

Maria smiled back at him. "Why don't I put the coffee on?" She said. "We can sit in my front room and keep the door open if you wish."

"Okay," he answered. "You probably make better coffee than I do anyway."

"Don't be so sure," she replied smiling back at him.

He returned a few minutes later, knocked on her open door and called out.

"I'm back. It's me Jim Anders."

Maria appeared through the doorway from her tiny kitchen. "Come in Mr. Anders."

"Please. Call me Jim." Then without hesitation asked, "May I call you Maria?"

"Sure," she replied. "The coffee's not quite ready."

"That's okay. We have to wait for the detectives anyway. Perhaps we can use this opportunity to get to know each other better. Since we live in the same building and on the same floor, we should at least know a bit more about someone we always see, but never seem to have the chance to talk to."

Maria motioned him toward a chair across from the coffee table, while she took a seat in her overstuffed love seat. She turned toward him. "Tell me Jim. Where are you from?" she asked starting the quiz.

"I'm from out west. I'm originally from Willow Creek. A tiny town you've probably never heard of. It's in Montana. I've worked several places and just recently took a job here as an accountant."

"So you moved in here until you can find someplace better?" Maria laughed.

"Well, sort of. I moved in here because it was available. It was the first place I looked at and as things turned out, I can walk to work from here."

"Really? Well, that's convenient, she replied. "Where do you work?"

"I'm with the accounting firm of Haywood, Smith & Wills. It's over on Fifth Avenue."

"Oh yes. I know where that is."

Just then she noticed the coffee pot had stopped perking. Maria got up and went into the kitchen. Jim looked around her small apartment and quickly learned how neat and in place everything seemed to be. Such a difference from his he thought.

Maria returned with a tray and two cups of steaming coffee. Also on the tray were two containers. One with sugar and the other a sugar substitute.

"I hope you don't need cream," she stated. "All I have is milk."

"No. I don't need anything."

Just then two men appeared at her doorway.

"Hello," one called out. "I'm Detective Jackobi. This is my partner Detective Ryan. We have a few questions."

The questions didn't take very long and finally Detective Jackobi said, "Okay. I guess both of you can go, but we may need to talk to you again."

As the two Detectives left Jim Anders turned to Maria.

"I guess we'd better be getting on to work. Sorry we never got to finish our coffee." "Yes," Maria replied without adding any other comments. As Jim reached the door of her apartment, he turned back in her direction.

"Would you have dinner with me tonight?" he asked boldly. "We could finish our conversation. There's a lovely restaurant about half way between here and where I work. We could walk there and back if you wouldn't mind."

Maria looked back at him hesitating for only a moment. She already knew he was very good looking and he certainly seemed to be nice.

She too was tired of eating alone. It would be a nice change. And besides, Agnes Benson could stop asking her if she'd met someone yet. Now she had.

Amble & David

By
Albert E. Farrar Jr.

Amble was apprehensive about seeing her brother. He'd just gotten out of jail and was coming to see her after more than 30 years. She'd never visited him in all the time he was in prison. Oh, he'd written a few time at first, but when she never responded, his letters stopped coming.

After all she blamed him for mom's death. How could she ever have anything to do with him? Sure he was here only brother and only sibling, but still . . . After the terrible thing he did that their mother took so very hard. Amble blamed him and could never forgive him.

Now he was coming to see her. Why she wondered? To ask for her forgiveness?

Well, he wasn't going to get it. Their relationship was over. She no longer had a brother.

Tomorrow was the day the letter in her hand said he planned to arrive.

Amble wondered if she should just be gone so she wouldn't have to face him. But no, she knew that wouldn't work. She had to come home sometime and he'd probably just wait.

She'd just gather up the courage to tell him face to face.

"David" she'd say. "You did a terrible thing and Mother never got over it. I hold you responsible for her death. I never want to see you again. Leave us alone."

That's what she'd tell him. She'd just gather up the courage, stand up straight and tall, and in her most forceful voice, tell him to "GO AWAY. I NEVER WANT TO SEE YOU AGAIN."

She wondered if she could do that. Would she have the courage? She must. She just must.

The next morning, Amble got up and did her usual morning things. Tom, her husband told here he would stay home if she wanted him too, but she told him "NO", she'd do this herself. It was better that way.

Her daughter Angie said she'd come over to be with her, but she told Angie, "NO" also.

It was a bit after 1p.m., when a taxi, pulled up in front of her home. Amble looked anxiously out the front window to see what he looked like after thirty years.

The taxi driver got out of the car and walked around to the back of the car and opened the trunk. She watched as the driver removed something and unfolded it to form a wheel chair. Then he opened the front door of the taxi and assisted his passenger into the chair.

Amble looked at the figure of the man, bent over with age and looking so frail. The taxi driver strapped the man into the chair and started pushing it up the walk way. She noticed the frail bent over figure never looked up, but just sat there, never moving.

"This can't be her brother David," she thought to herself. He was always so active as a younger man.

The door bell rang and Amble took the few steps to the front door. Her hand reached hesitantly for the knob. Turning it, she pulled the door open. The frail figure hardly moved as the driver asked.

"Mrs. Amble Saunders?"

"Yes." she replied.

"I was told to bring this gentleman here and to wait for him," he said.

Amble looked down at the body in the chair. He had not moved from his slightly bent over position.

"Bring him in," she instructed.

Closing the door behind them, Amble walked around in front of the chair and looked down at the figure of a man obviously ill with some kind of physical disability.

He did not look up. She bent down so as to better see his face.

His eyes looked up at her from his bent over position.

"Hello Sis," he said in a frail sounding voice.

Amble was stunned at the sight of her brother. She never even considered he might arrive in this condition. She'd expected him to arrive, stride up to the front door and greet her as if nothing ever happened. But No! Here he was almost on death's door.

"David." she finally said stunned by his appearance.

She saw a half smile on his face as he said.

"Bet you never thought you'd see me like this?"

She was momentarily speechless.

"What happened?"

"Doctor's say I have only month to live. Something's taken over my body. I just had to see you Sis."

"Oh David!" She reached down to touch him. "I'm so sorry."

"It's okay Sis," he replied.

"How long have you been like this?"

"Not long. Maybe a year. It happened all at once."

Amble started to cry. She was suddenly overcome by the sight of her brother. Tears ran down her face as she fell onto her knees and reached out to touch her brother.

"Don't cry Sis," he said. "It's okay."

The taxi driver broke in.

"I have to get him back to the hospital. He insisted on coming and the Doctors said he could only be gone for an hour off the machines."

Amble looked up at the sound of the voice.

"I just had to see you Sis," her brother said.

"If only I'd known," she replied.

"I figured you never wanted to see me." David said in a voice barely audible.

"But I had to try."

Tears fell from her cheeks onto the front of her dress as she held his hands.

"Oh David," was all she could utter?

In a few minutes he was back in the taxi and as it drove away from the curb, a new round of tears overcame her and she collapsed sobbing into a nearby chair.

David passed away two months later, but his sister was there by his side every day.

A Detective Dilemma

By
Albert E. Farrar Jr.

Detective Skip McIver chewed on the end of his pencil. A serial Killer was on the prowl in his city, and he was no closer to solving it five murders later, than he was after the first one. He knew the mayor would have his behind, but he couldn't really do anything. Evidence was almost non existent.

From across the room he heard someone call his name.

"Hey Skip. We just got the photo of the latest murder scene. It's a bit fuzzy but at least we have a photo of the killer this time."

"Let me see it," Skip commanded the other detective. Skip looked at the photo and discovered detective Smith was right. It was fuzzy and difficult to really see clearly the face. It was another of those security cameras that didn't really take good pictures. Why business owners who had these camera's installed didn't spend a few extra bucks and get one that took really good photo's he would never understand.

"I can't tell who this is," Skip said to the other detective. "How are we supposed to be able to recognize who this might be?"

"The photo lab is trying to make it clearer. Maybe they will have some success."

"Don't count on it. They weren't able to improve the photo from a robbery last week. They probably won't be able to improve this one either"

Skip took the magnifying glass from his desk drawer and peered through it to see if the photo would become easier for him to distinguish.

It did not. Still, as he continued to look, there was something about the hazy photo from the security camera that looked familiar to him. There was something about that face through all the lines and distortion of the photo that looked a bit like a face he'd seen before, but it wasn't clear. It was too unclear to be able to tell just who it might be.

Finally he put the magnifier away and set the photo down on his desk to wait for perhaps a clearer photo from the photo lab.

The day ground to an end and Skip McIver picked up the photo for one last look before turning off his desk lamp and going home for the day. He hoped that his wife Mabel would have prepared a good dinner. He was especially hungry today for some reason. Skip hoped it would be better than the Spanish rice she served last night. Mabel knew he didn't like Spanish rice and yet every once in awhile she insisted on serving it. If she liked it, why couldn't she just fix some for herself and something else for him? But no, she'd fix it for the whole family.

Shaun, his son didn't like it either and would always make an excuse to eat with a friend when he knew his mother was fixing that dish. Maybe Skip should find a friend to go eat with, but he knew that wouldn't work. Maybe Shaun could get away with it, but he was sure he couldn't. Mabel would surely think he was seeing another woman. That's the way her mind worked even though he'd never cheated on her and she knew it.

"Oh, well," he muttered. "I guess it's just part of being married."

At breakfast the next morning, his wife Mabel said, "You were up last night. Couldn't you sleep well? Was something from work bothering you?"

"I don't know," Skip replied. He didn't remember being up last night. The last thing he remembered was thinking about that photo and then waking up this morning when the alarm went off.

"You don't remember being up last night?" she asked.

"No." he replied.

Well, the breakfast was good this morning and the dinner last night was super. Mabel knew he didn't like Spanish rice and she'd always fix his favorite meal the very next night for dinner. I guess she knew how to win him back and keep him happy. Maybe that's why their twenty year marriage survived this long. It wasn't always easy with the hours he had to work sometimes, but she was a good person and he loved her in spite of her feeling it necessary to fix that Spanish rice dinner once in awhile.

"Hey Skip," the detective said when he arrived in the office. We had another robbery and shooting last night. This time I think the victim is going to survive. And by the way," he continued. "Here is the new photo from the photo lab." He was laughing as he spoke.

"What's the matter?" Skip asked. "What's so funny?"

"This clarified photo of the robber?"

"Yes?" Skip answered in a questioning voice.

The detective replied. "The killer looks just like you."

Love in A Frozen Church Yard

By
Albert E. Farrar Jr.

It was the coldest winter the natives could ever remember. It seemed like it would never end. Snow was piled up as high as any of the natives ever saw. The small town of westerfield was off the main highway in the farm lands of the Midwest. It was so small there wasn't even a post office. Their mail was delivered by truck to the general store five days a week about ten a.m. This was the first time anyone could recall that the mail truck had not come in three days.

"No mail again today?" Old Jacob Stubens asked the store clerk after he'd trudged through the snow that at times was almost up to his waist.

"No Jacob." Hazel the store clerk said as she huddled close to the old pot bellied stove in the middle of her tiny store.

"I haven't seen a customer since day before yesterday when Oscar Watts found his way here to get a few things his wife sent him for. He was cussing all the way here and I'll bet he was cussing all the way home about her sending him out in weather like this. Good thing he and I live close by."

"When do you think it's going to break Hazel?" Jacob asked.

"I don't know. The radio man said it would be a few more days for sure."

"I hope everyone has enough food and heat to last them," he replied.

"I do too. Do you need anything Jacob as long as you're here?"

"I guess it wouldn't hurt to take a few things back with me. Have you got any coffee Hazel to warm up my bones?"

"Oh sure Jacob. I'm sorry. I should have offered you some as soon as you came in."

He stood close to the old stove trying to thaw out while Hazel went to the back of the store to get him some hot coffee.

"You know what?" Jacob said when she returned.

"What?" she asked as she handed him a cup of steaming coffee.

"I worry about old Jim Smith. You know he always went up to his wife's grave by the church every day. You don't suppose he'd try and do that in this kind of weather do you?"

"I wouldn't think so." Hazel answered.

"Have you seen him since this weather started?"

"He was in the day before, but no. I haven't seen him since."

Hazel thought a moment and then asked.

"You don't really think he'd try and go there in this snow do you?"

"I don't know. He was always pretty faithful about visiting her every day."

"How can we find out?" Hazel asked.

Jacob thought for a moment and then said.

"Do you suppose I should try and make my way down to his house and see if he's there?"

"I hate to have you try and do that. You live close to the store here, but he's almost a mile down the road. I don't think you could make there and back Jacob. You'd better not try."

Just then Levi Johnson came through the door of the store.

"What are you doing out here Levi?" Jacob asked.

"The Mrs. wanted me to get some fuel oil for the lantern. We run out last night. As long as I'm here I might as well get a few groceries too."

"I see you made your horse bring you." Jacob said.

"Yeh! I didn't think I could make it walking. But Dolly's got long legs. I'm going to put her right back in the barn when I get home. It's cold inside there also but I'll give her extra oats and hay. She'll be all right."

"Say Levi. You're pretty close to Jim Smith's place aren't you?

"Yes. He's just beyond my place, why?"

"Well, we've been worried about him. He goes to the cemetery every day to visit his wife Wilma's grave and we are worried he might have gone during this storm."

"Oh, I don't think he'd do that. Old Jim is smarter than to go out in this kind of weather." Levi answered.

"Well, I don't know. He goes there every day, faithful as can be."

"Yeah! But he wouldn't go in weather like this."

"We're kind of worried. I saw him the day before the storm, but I've not seen him since."

"He's probably just like most of us. Holed up in his place until this clears up."

"I was thinking." Jacob said. "Since you've got Dolly and you have to pass right by the church graveyard on the way home, maybe you could take a look."

"I didn't see anyone up there on my way in, but of course I wasn't lookin. Tell you what. I'll look up there on my way back. The graveyard is in front of the church and since it's all on a sloping piece of ground, I should be able to see if anyone is up there."

"With all this snow, it might be hard to tell unless you actually go up there off the road." Jacob said.

"Well, I don't know if Dolly and me can make it up there. It was tough enough just getting in here."

"You need to try Levi." Hazel said.

"He wouldn't go there. Jim's smarter than to try and make it to the graveyard in this kind of weather." Levi said. "I'll look when I go by. If I think we can make it up there, maybe we'll try."

Levi took his groceries and lamp fuel, mounted old Dolly and headed back the way he came.

"I think I should go home." Jacob said. "Now that I've warmed up, I can make it back."

Two days later the snow started to melt. On Saturday the mail truck made it through to deliver the mail and the people of Westerfield started to move around. Hazel's store was full of people wanting to re-supply their needs. Levi showed up just before noon.

Jacob was standing by the stove as usual drinking his cup of coffee, while Hazel was busy with the many customers.

"Levi." Jacob said. "Did you ever get up to the cemetery to check on Jim Smith?"

"I couldn't get old Dolly up there," he replied, "But I went to his house after I got home and gave Dolly some rest and plenty of food.

"And?" Jacob asked.

"I made it to his house just up the road from my place. He was there. He's just fine but when I told him why I came, he started to cry. He told me he tried to make it to his wife's grave, but he couldn't get there. Too much snow. He said he'd promised her he would visit her every day and he just couldn't make it.

Told me a couple of time he almost gave up and thought of just lying down in the snow and giving up. He said that maybe that way they'd be together again.

"I put my arm around him and told him Wilma wouldn't want him to do that. I stayed with him quite awhile and we talked and eventually he calmed down a bit. When I left, I felt pretty sure he was okay.

Anyway, I think he'll be okay. He should be able to get up there by tomorrow. Once he can do that, he'll be all right."

"I sure hope so." Jacob said. "I sure hope so."

They found his body next to his wife's grave the next morning, frozen. Old Jim just couldn't stay away any longer. Apparently he'd made it up there the night before and stayed with her all night in the last of the freezing temperatures. There was evidence of a small fire all burned out next to his body.

The Twisted Clover

By
Albert E. Farrar Jr.

This is the story of a twisted piece of clover in the front yard home of John Smith. He was twisted between a myriad of other clovers, so much so that he was unable to stand up straight. The only good thing about his position was that he was always warm. Now that was good in the winter but in the summer he really suffered. It was difficult to breath.

When John Smith would cut the grass, the mower blades would always miss his delicate head. All the other clovers around him would get their heads chopped off, and by the time it was mowing time again, they had grown up around him once more, and he would be safe once again.

Then there was the fertilizer. Boy that was terrible tasting stuff. Old twisted clover would gag and choke, and he'd always pray for rain. Thank goodness old Mr. Smith would always water right after and that helped wash the smell and taste away.

He wished he could live someplace far away. Perhaps on a high hill top so he could look down over all the land with trees, and animals and perhaps even a small stream so he could watch the fish swimming up to spawn.

But no, here he was in old Mr. Smith's front yard. What chance did he have?

"I'm stuck here," he'd say to himself. "I'm stuck here all my life. Pretty soon the winter will come and the grass will turn brown and me and the other clover will be gone until next year. Then come spring we'll all be back and I'll probably be in the same situation."

Then one day as the wind started to blow and the temperatures dropped, old Mr. Smith came into the front yard with a funny looking machine. He turned it on and the ground began to vibrate. Clover stretched as far up as he could. All he could see was the ground being lifted up. The machine came closer and closer. It passed right next to him. Then it turned around and was heading straight toward him. Twisted clover tried to duck down, bit it ran right over him. It dug up the ground all around. His roots were town loose from the soft good dirt.

A little while later he was scooped up and hauled away in a big truck. They went for a long ride to a far away place. Finally the truck stopped and the men got out and tossed all the chunks of grass and clover onto the ground. He was alone now as were the other clovers and grass. Soon it was winter. Twisted clover went to sleep thinking this was the end.

Much later twisted clover woke up. It was warm and he could feel the sun all around. Some of the other clovers were also awake. He stretched his leafs and looked around. He was on a hill. There were animals on the hill walking around. At the bottom of the hill he could see a stream.

His dream had come true. He was where he always wanted to be.

But wait. There was a big animal moving his way.

"Stop Mr. Animal," he cried. "Don't come any closer. Stop," he called once more. But the animal walked right over the top of twisted clover and there he stopped.

"Go away animal," twisted clover shouted.

But the animal did not. Instead, all of a sudden something fell right on top of twisted clover's head.

"I can't breath," he shouted. "What is that terrible smell? It sure stinks."

A Moment of Panic

By
Albert E. Farrar Jr.

The train from Canada was late, but he dragged his two pieces of luggage across the marble floor of New York's Grand Central Station looking for a place to sit until it was time for his connection to Los Angeles. As he looked around he noticed that empty places on the wooden benches were few and far between. There were even a few men sitting on the marble floor, apparently waiting for their train to be called.

Then against the far wall between the restrooms he noticed a small bench with one spot still open. Sitting on one end was a young lady, all alone. He headed in that direction since he wasn't too keen on taking one of the many places on the floor with the others.

"Excuse me. Would you mind if I shared this bench with you?" he asked.

She looked up at him with a smile as lovely as he'd seen in a long time. He noticed her blonde hair, red lips and sparkling eyes. Her skin was beautiful and un-blemished. Why she was alone he couldn't understand.

"No, I don't mind," she replied.

"Thank you. I just came off the train from Canada and we were delayed several times on our way here. I am so tired of being on that train and now I have to wait for another one."

She smiled but did not answer.

He sat his luggage beside the bench, took a deep breath and then turning toward her asked.

"Been waiting here long?"

"No," she answered.

"I'm waiting for a train to Los Angeles. I hate doing it, but its part of my job. I was hired to write a story about train travel today and compare it against train travel fifty years ago. In order to do that, I figured I needed to actually make a long train trip."

He paused a brief moment and then said. "I think I'll fly back after I get out there."

When she didn't answer, he asked "Where are you headed?"

"I'm on my way to Miami," she said.

"It's lovely down there. Have you ever been there before?"

"No," came her reply.

"I spent last winter there," he hesitated and then went on. "Well, not all winter; actually just a month. I think I might like to retire there one day. May I ask why you're going there?

She turned to face him for the first time and with a smile on her face said. "I'm going to visit my Aunt. She lives there. I just finished college and I'm taking a break before I start looking for a job."

He loved the sound of her voice. It was the first time she'd spoken enough for him to really get to know what it sounded like.

"Are you going to look for work down there?"

"No, I don't think so."

Changing the subject, he asked. "What do you like to do for excitement?"

Again she looked in his direction and smiled as she answered. "I'm a skier. I love to ski."

"Really?" he replied. "I've done a bit of skiing in Canada. Are you good?"

She laughed for the first time before she replied. "Oh, pretty good I think. I tried out for the Olympics last year."

"No kidding," he exclaimed. "You must be pretty good then."

"I guess not," she answered. "I didn't qualify. I missed the cut by sixteen seconds. I was second alternate but I never got a chance to participate."

"I'm sorry. I guess I'd better never invite you to go skiing with me. I'm afraid I'd be embarrassed."

She laughed at his response and he went on. "I can see why you might not want to live in Miami. They don't have a lot of snow."

They both laughed once more at his remark.

"Does your gentleman friend ski?"

"Oh, I don't have a gentleman friend. I've been too busy with school and my skiing. When I get back from Florida, I'll find a job and continue to practice and maybe next time I'll try again."

"If I were a judge, you'd win," he commented

They both laughed again and she answered. "I'll have to request you to be a judge at the next Olympics."

He couldn't take his eyes off her. The longer he looked and they talked, the more he felt he would like to know her a whole lot better.

Just then the loud speaker interrupted their conversation.

"Am track express train number forty three now boarding on track seven for Washington D.C., Richmond Virginia, Raleigh North Carolina, Savannah Georgia, Jacksonville, Orlando and Miami, Florida. All aboard."

"That's me," she said. "I've got to go," and she stood up.

He stood up with her, shook her hand and said. "I've really enjoyed our short time together. Best wishes on your next Olympic try."

She smiled and said. "Thanks. Good luck on your train story."

She turned and pulling her piece of luggage, headed toward the loading platform.

He watched her walk across the large station waiting room and disappear through the doors leading to the trains.

A bit dejected he slumped down on the bench, knowing he wasn't going to see her again. She was the first young lady to make his heart pump a bit faster in a much longer time than he could remember.

"Why didn't I find out if I could see her after this trip? I didn't even get her name."

He sat there for a moment and then said out loud. "You dumb dodo! You idiot."

Instantly, he stood up, leaving his luggage by the bench and ran toward the door leading toward the loading platform.

"Which is the train to Miami?" he asked the station attendant.

"I need to see your ticket," the attendant ordered.

"I don't have a ticket. I just need to find someone on that train."

"If you don't have a ticket you can't go over there," the attendant replied.

"But I need to find someone. I forgot to get her name."

"I'm sorry, but you can't go over there. The train is almost ready to leave."

He stood there looking toward the several trains, all waiting to leave.

"Please. I need to find her."

"Sorry," the station attendant answered.

Dejected he turned back toward the doors leading inside to the waiting room.

Slumping down onto the bench, he put his head into his hands and leaning forward he started to berate himself for being so stupid. He sat there for several minutes staring down at the floor.

Suddenly he heard a familiar voice. "I'm glad you're still here."

He looked up and there she stood, staring down at him, as beautiful a young lady as he'd ever laid eyes on.

"I was hoping you might still be here," she said.

"What about your train?" he asked.

"I'm going to catch a later one. I couldn't leave without knowing your name. I'd like to see you again after your trip and mine."

"I ran out to the platform trying to catch you," he said.

"I know," she answered. "I saw you and it was then that I realized that I wanted to see you again, so I got off the train and came back."

He looked up at the station ceiling and murmured, "Thank you God."

He took her hands in his and said.

"By the way my name is Jeffrey."

"I'm Monica," she replied and they sat back down on the bench to visit awhile longer, completely unaware of any activity in the huge train station.

Christmas Story Starter

By
Albert E. Farrar Jr.

Johnny shook the last coin from his piggy bank. $2.67—that was all the money he had to buy Christmas gifts for his mother, father, sister, and grandmother.

What was he going to do? He knew that was only about 66 cents for each of them. What could he buy each of them for just 66 cents? He knew he'd have to try.

Johnny put the coins in his pocket and headed out the door and down the street toward the big store a mile away from his home. It was cold outside, but he knew enough to wear his heavy coat, gloves and with a scarf around his neck and a wool cap that covered his ears and head, he was off determined to find something with his meager funds.

The snow had stopped falling, but it was still several inches thick on the ground. His footprints were the only ones he could see. No one else had ventured out this morning. The sky was now clear and the breeze, though light, was cold. He trudged on and on heading toward the store. Soon he could see some of the buildings and he knew it wouldn't be long before he would be warm again inside of the biggest building of them all.

On he trudged still making new footprints in the unmarked snow. He'd passed no one during his long walk. Johnny was glad he was getting close because in spite of his warm clothing, he was starting to feel the cold that had penetrated his warm coat. It was the one his father bought him a few months before to protect him from the coming winter weather.

As he got closer he could now see a few people on the sidewalk. Soon he was there and he was inside the big store where he could get warm while he looked for something, anything that he could buy for 66 cents.

Johnny walked up and down aisles looking at one item and then another. Finally, there on a table in front of him was a stack of ladies aprons.

That's it, his mind said. Grandma and mother could each use one of those. There was a big sale sign standing right in the middle of the table. It said. HALF PRICE!

Johnny picked up a pretty flowered apron and thought. *Grandma would like this one!* He looked at the price tag that hung from one corner. $1.49 it said. Johnny knew that half price still meant it cost seventy-five cents. That was a full nine cents more than he could spend on each person.

Maybe I can get dad and sis something for less, he thought. I could find something for 57 cents for each of them, I'm sure I can.

He reached into his pocket for the money and was surprised to learn there were only two coins there. Johnny pulled them out to learn they were pennies. Quickly he reached into the other pocket of his trousers and finding no other coins, quickly checked all the pockets of his coat and shirt. Alas, there were no coins anywhere. Then reaching back into the first pocket with his fingers, Johnny discovered a small hole in the bottom of his pants pocket.

"Oh no," he uttered. "I've got a hole in my pocket. All the money must have fallen out. What am I going to do? I only have two pennies."

He stood there for a moment and suddenly coming to the realization that he had no money to buy Christmas presents for his family, he dejectedly placed the aprons back on the table, turned and walked outside to sit on a bench placed near the front door.

Sitting there for a few moments thinking about the loss of his meager amount of money, he started to cry.

A few people went in and a few came out of the store, but none of them stopped to see what was wrong.

Then from the nearby corner came a man dressed in a familiar red suit. He had a bushy white beard, a red hat and black boots.

"What's the matter young man?" the deep gruff voice asked.

"I lost my money to buy Christmas presents," Johnny said with tears still running down his cheeks.

"Oh my," The man said. "That's very bad. Was it a lot of money?"

"It was $2.76. I was going to buy presents for grandma, my mother and my dad and my sister. It's all the money I had. I walked over a mile just to get here and I think the money fell out of a hole in my pocket. Now I can't buy any Christmas presents."

Johnny started to cry once more.

"Now, Now," The man in the red suit said. "Maybe Santa can help. Do you know what you were going to buy?"

"I found two nice aprons," Johnny said through the tears and choking voice. They were just perfect for my grandma and mother. I don't know yet what I was getting my dad or sister."

"Let's go inside and see what we can find. Perhaps Santa can help. Show me the two aprons that you wanted to buy Johnny."

They walked to the table and Johnny picked up the two aprons and handed them to the person in the red suit.

"Here they are," he said. The Santa dressed man looked and said. "They are very nice Johnny. I'll remember and I'll tell my elves about them. Now let's go see if we can find something for you sister and father."

As Johnny turned to head toward the clothing department for young ladies, the person in the red suit motioned to a nearby sales person and then followed Johnny to another part of the store. After looking around for a few minutes, Johnny said.

"There's nothing here I can get for my sister. I only had 57 cents to spend on her. But now I don't have anything."

"Do you see anything at all she might like?" Santa asked.

"I know she'd like that sweater over there, but it five dollars."

"Well, let's look for something for your father. What would he like?"

"Mama says he needs some new work shirts, but I don't have any money now."

"Well, Johnny how about if Santa loans you the money? You can pay me back by being good this next year?"

"You'd do that?" Johnny asked a look of surprise and hope on his face.

"Sure. I've done that before to some of my special young people. Maybe if you're good all year, Santa might even say you don't have to pay him back."

"I'd be good. I promise," Johnny replied excitedly.

Johnny trudged home not even noticing the cold and the snow that was now falling once again.

Christmas morning after breakfast, the family gathered around the big decorated tree to start opening their presents.

"Here Grandma," Johnny said. "This one's for you and it's from me," he said proudly.

Grandma carefully unwrapped the paper holding the small package and inside she found not one beautiful apron exactly like the one Johnny picked out, but two others equally as beautiful."

Johnny was surprised because he expected only the one apron Santa had promised.

Then Johnny handed his mother her present next and also was equally surprised to find three beautiful aprons for her.

Johnny's sister opened her gift to find a beautiful sweater just like the one he saw at the store. Johnny was again surprised by his sister's gift.

Then his father opened his present to find three wonderful work shirts in different colors.

"Johnny." His mother asked. "Where did you get the money to buy all these presents?

Johnny smiled. "I talked to Santa and I promised to be good this year if he'd help me get some nice presents for my family."

That night as Johnny lay in bed looking out his window, he noticed the sky had cleared and there were stars everywhere. He got up from his bed and walked to the window and looking up into the heavens, he said, "Thank you Santa for making this the best Christmas ever."

Out there in the dark sky, he saw one very bright star and Johnny noticed it was blinking right at him. For just a second that blinking star looked just like the face of Santa.

Beverly's Stories

Beverly Anderson

Beverly was born in Nebraska and spent her childhood in Eastern Oregon. Following her first marriage, she traveled the world with her Air Force husband and three precious sons. She was a full-time mom, but gained a wealth of experience through part time jobs and volunteering.

Beverly began writing by delving into the field of memoir. She branched out to poetry, fiction short stories and writing a weekly article for her church newsletter. This will be her second printed work.

She wishes to thank her friends and fellow writers in her critique groups for their unending encouragement and advice. She also thanks her husband for his patience and support. She looks forward to finishing her first novel and continuing her memoir that is ongoing. Writing has become her passion.

Heaven, Coming and Going

By
Beverly Anderson

A baby girl sent right from God.
She arrived in early spring.
God gave our prayers a nod.
And church bells began to ring.

She brought a ray of light.
To Great Great Grandma Ruth.
Very old, and poor of sight.
Our Grandma knew the truth.

One now entering our world.
One getting ready to leave.
Fingers so old they curled.
A new baby—we shouldn't grieve.

It's sad, they had less than a year.
Indeed they spent it well.
Bonding—intimate and dear.
Their love had cast a spell.

Thank God for our precious girl.
She's everything we wanted.
What a blessing, what a pearl.
In our hearts she's firmly planted.

Now our loving Grandma's gone
She went on to her reward.
She was with us for oh so long.
But our memories are safely stored.

A darling girl she held, so sweet.
The sign of a new day.
Now the circle is complete.
And both had found their way.

Journey to Peace

By
Beverly Anderson

I wasn't very brave when it came to adventuring in strange places. Heck, I always thought a monster lived under my bed, ready to grab my legs when I stepped close. That's why I ran from the middle of the room and jumped into bed at night.

Annie was so insistent though and I knew I needed to be brave for her sake. She was my best friend and I wasn't about to leave her in the well.

I clung to the rope and slowly lowered myself down the dark, damp hole.

"Are you coming?" she asked as little pieces fell from the sides of the well. I never heard them hit bottom and that was scary.

"Yes, I'm on my way," I said in a trembling voice.

Suddenly the rope slipped through my hands and my legs kicked out and hit a ledge. I grabbed a dead branch and managed to keep from falling farther into the well.

"Annie, where are you, I got caught on the ledge."

"I'm just below, let go and you'll drop to where I am. It won't hurt; it's not far."

How did I ever let Annie get me into this mess? I closed my eyes, took my life in my hands and dropped into the abyss. I was going to die. Then a miracle happened, my feet touched something soft like a mattress. I rolled over from the impact and opened my eyes. Much to my shock, there were little white beings with silver wings and beautiful smiles on their faces flying around a big, gorgeous room. Iridescent lights swirled around the beings as they frivolously tossed baby birds into the air. The tiny, humming birds fluttered their wings and landed on ledges around the walls of the well. Fountains spewed water glittering with silver and gold sprinkles as the water cascaded down the walls of the room. It dissipated before it hit the floor.

"Annie, what in the world is this? I have never seen anything like it."

"Yes, that's why I wanted you to come down. Isn't it just the most beautiful thing you have ever seen? I've no idea what it is or why, but you had to see it. Can you imagine what our parents will say when we tell them about it? Maybe we better not; they'll take put us in a mental institution."

Then a tall figure dressed in a white robe appeared. It had a pale pink flower where a face would be. The flower was covered with dew drops. Her arms were a feathery type of green leaves. She spoke in a breathless voice.

"This place is only in your dreams. When you leave here, it will disappear, but you will always take it with you in your memory. When you are having a bad day, you can come to this place. Please enjoy yourselves for the next few moments, and then you will have to grab the rope and go back to the world.

"You may call this place; Peace."

Blue Gold

By
Beverly Anderson

For me, climbing into a favorite pair of blue jeans is more satisfying than eating a hot fudge sundae. Give me a comfortable pair of jeans any day, or evening for that matter. In the 1940's when I was a little girl, jeans were worn only on the farm, or under a dress for warmth. Jeans had to be removed as soon as we walked into school. I wore mine under my dress and as soon as I got there I hung them in the cloak room with my coat. They zipped up the side.

I loved my jeans. I wore them as I played in the hay stack and crawled on the freshly mown lawn looking for four leaf clovers. My pockets were always full. I carried special rocks, a hanky, a coin or two, a note from a friend and a piece or two of candy.

By the time I went to high school, jeans were more accepted everywhere. Dresses were worn to a prom, church or if you were having a school picture taken. Of course there were Jantzen sweaters and Pendleton skirts, but that's another story.

One of the best things about jeans was they didn't have to be washed as often. The stains seemed to disappear into the denim. They never needed ironing. Dresses always did. Another thing, they didn't show too much when you sat down as dresses might. A wind storm, a severe problem when wearing a dress, was no problem for a girl in jeans.

Jeans have been around since the 1880s and at first cost $1.50. A similar pair today would sell for $39.00. They were worn by workers in factories during WWII. Beginning in the 1950s, jeans were in great demand both here and around the world. They were very expensive outside the United States so some foreign travelers filled their suitcases with them to take home. In Russia, during the Cold War, jeans were more valuable than money and almost anything could be acquired for a pair.

During the 1950s I became a teenager and I still loved jeans. The style was to roll a wide cuff just under the knee cap. We were so cool! They looked even cooler when they were worn with our dad's white shirts, un-tucked, sleeves rolled to the elbow, collar turned up.

Jeans in the sixties were painted with peace signs, hearts and squiggles in many different colors. The new jeans for women had a zipper in the front, just like men's.

Then in the seventies, dark blue denim took a back seat to faded blue bell bottoms, the latest rage for the hippie generation. The eighties jeans were stone washed, and teens sprayed them with bleach to make them turn white. Some girls wore theirs so tight, they had to lie on the bed to get the zipper up.

Over the years, jeans have changed a great deal. There are low rise waists, flared or straight legs, crops and shorts. Pockets come plain, embroidered, with flaps, or no pockets at all. There are dark blue ones, faded blue ones, or upscale ones with ragged holes. There are as many labels as there are styles. You can't beat the reputation of the old standbys though. Levi's top the list with Lee a safe second and Wranglers third. Designer labels are too many to mention, but the choice is yours and so is the price.

Now, jeans are considered smart for men—or women. They are accepted everywhere worldwide. Men wear them with an open collared shirt and a nice sport jacket. Women wear tight jeans, a leather jacket hoop earrings and carry a designer purse. The latest rage is jean leggings and pockets right in the material.

Me, I'll take my old farm jeans any day. Don't ask me when I washed them last—I guess I wouldn't remember.

Daily Moon Award

By
Beverly Anderson

I'm sitting in the most beautiful dining room in the most elegant city on Earth. I'm waiting to collect my award for being the youngest, old person. First let me tell you how I happened to be here.

The dining room is at the top of the International Butterfly Castle, located just outside Cut Bank, Montana. You wouldn't believe the beauty of this area. Seattle/Tacoma became overwhelmed with River People around 2020. The water rose gradually in all the local rivers due to an unusual amount of rainfall. Over time the population living close to the water developed fins and fishtails. Normal, land-loving humans began to feel like outsiders. We took matters in our own hands and made plans to move.

My husband and I heard there was an Eden-like area near Cut Bank, Montana and why not see what it is all about. We packed our helicopter, left the River People to their water world and took off. We landed outside Cut Bank, then stayed the night at an upscale Motel 64. After sleeping an hour, which had become the norm, we were escorted to the Castle by the prettiest hostesses this side of International Falls, MN. They appeared totally nude, but body parts weren't visible. They were dressed in the new spray-on material that warms in winter and cools in summer. The next time I go to Nordwalls I'll see if they have any left. For those of you that hadn't heard, Nordstrom and Walmart joined forces in late 2018 and ran all other stores out of business.

When we arrived at the Butterfly Castle, large butterflies flitted down from the dining room and lifted us on wings, through fluffy white clouds to a gold gilded, all glass enclosed room. We were carried through diaphanous sliding doors. Fresh food from all over the world, was served from invisible, miniature silver platters that popped up onto white marble tables, with soft Egyptian Cotton hammocks swinging at the sides. We entered the room and immediately slid into the comfortable hammocks.

After this divine repast, we left the dining room, by the same method we had arrived. The need to explore the possibility of finding a permanent place to settle down consumed us and we couldn't wait to explore our new found paradise. Finally we found our perfect spot. We bought a plot of ground nearby and what a steal! For a mere million-and-a-half we got four hundred square feet. We constructed our dream home from recycled volcanic ash and oil spill held together with recycled plastic milk jugs. We loved our six floor skyscraper home and felt good about doing our part for ecology.

Now here's the reason I got the award. During the building our dream home I enjoyed taking a break and going to the Cut Bank River to play with the children. They looked and acted young, but seemed to have the wisdom of the aged. As I spent more time with those children, the younger I felt. Soon I started to look young. One day in the local newspaper, The Daily Moon, an article mentioned a prize for the youngest old person. Why not apply I thought. My real age of ninety-five had morphed to my new age of fifteen. I knew I'd have an excellent chance of winning.

Guess what? I won! They invited my husband and me to come and accept it and that's why we're here in this beautiful dining room where I plan to spend more time encouraging others to come to the Cut Bank River and play with the children and me.

Sam's Night Fright

By
Beverly Anderson

"Dang, Jenny, you did it again!" Sam moaned, as his old seventy-nine Ford clanked and ground to a halt. It was past midnight. He wanted to make it home so he could sleep in his own bed, but no, Jenny had to have one of her spells. It seemed like a good name when he bought her at the local Ford garage twenty years ago. Now her name seemed more like a curse word.

As he drove home from his last call as a traveling salesman for Mountain Clear Water, he found himself stuck in a small town in the middle of nowhere. Up ahead was a neon motel sign. He'd walk there, get a room for the night and see if Jenny could be fixed in the morning. He was too tired to mess with her engine now.

He opened the squeaky door of the motel office. The old woman at the desk was sound asleep with an inky, black cat in her lap. Neither moved. He politely patted the bell on the desk. Nothing. He cleared his throat and slapped the bell.

"Uh, uhm, can I he'p ya'?" she asked as she tried to stand. The cat fell from her lap and stretched, giving the intruder a cat-eyed look.

"Yes ma'am, I need a room for the night. My car died down the road and I'll have to get it fixed in the morning."

"That'll be fifty dollars, paid in advance. It's the policy. We don't take no credit cards."

Sam sucked in his breath. Fifty dollars for this old dump? He had no choice. He paid with three twenties. She handed him the change and the key to room #213. "The room is up the stairs. At the landing take a right. It's on your left." She settled back in her chair and dropped her head.

The stairs were dimly lit. Near the top he tripped on a loose tread and dropped his suitcase. It bumped all the way to the bottom.

The old woman yelled, "What's going on up there? People are tryin' ta sleep don't cha' know? Quiet down."

Sam hurried back down the stairs and retrieved the suitcase. The hallway had no more light than the stairs and it had a dank aroma. After looking at each door, he found #213 and inserted the key. It was rusty and took some time to get it to work. Strange.

He found the light switch and glanced around. The room was small, but adequate for one night. After several attempts to lock the door he moved a chair against it and set his suitcase on the floor. Then he checked the bathroom. It too was tiny, but clean. He looked at the bed which had a deep indentation in the middle. At least he wouldn't fall out. As was his habit since childhood, he looked underneath. Nothing, or so it seemed. It was too dark to get a good look.

Sam breathed a sigh and opened his suitcase. He would brush his teeth and go right to bed. He took a step toward the bathroom and the door closed. What? He tentatively opened the door, then stepped inside. The light went out. As he reached for the switch, it came on again. Why didn't he just grab his stuff and get out of this eerie place, but he was tired to the bone and besides he had already paid the un-refundable fifty bucks. Dang.

He brushed his teeth. When he came out of the bathroom, he was startled to see the inky black cat lying in the middle of the bed. The door was shut, the window too. It wasn't possible, yet there it was. It looked up at him and yawned. No way would he sleep with a cat. He grabbed the cat, opened the door and tossed it out. The cat didn't seem the least bit surprised. Sam suddenly had the shakes. He had never experienced such weird things. Maybe he was over tired. That was it—he was just tired.

A light that wasn't there before was shining through the only window. He looked out. Jenny was in the parking lot with the hazard lights flashing. She gleamed as if she had just been through a car wash, even though Sam remembered how dirty she was from all the driving. He couldn't believe it. He wiped his eyes and looked again. She was gone. Garbage cans lined the street, silhouetted from the dim street light.

He'd had enough. He didn't care if he lost his fifty bucks. He would walk back to Jenny, if she was still there and sleep in the back seat all night. This was just too spooky. He had to get out of here. He grabbed his suitcase from the floor. What was the matter with it? It was too light. He opened it and there was nothing inside. No computer, no pajamas, no nothing. It was all there before. What happened? Sam ran out of the room with his empty suitcase in his hand. At the front desk, the old woman was gone. A gorgeous young gal was standing there.

"Hi, honey, don't you just love our cute little hotel? We had such fun decorating it and making it a place of peace and harmony. Did you have a good sleep?"

"What is going on here? Are you messing with my mind? Nothing has gone right since I walked in the door. I want my stuff that was in my suitcase and I want my money back. You hear me? I want my stuff!"

"Now calm down, honey, we can make it right. Part of our service is to clean everything for you. We even cleaned your computer. You just have a seat and you'll have your stuff in a jiffy. We value our customers and want to send them out feeling rested, relaxed and everything clean and renewed."

"Don't call me honey. What do you mean you cleaned my computer?"

"We cleaned everything off of it. That's one of our special services. Now you have a spotless clean machine. No files to clutter it up. It's just like brand new and so are your clothes. Here you go honey." She pulled a box with all of his stuff from under the counter. "You come back and see us real soon. Okay, snooks?"

Sam was shaking so hard he could hardly talk. He grabbed the box. "I'm out of here. You are all a bunch of loonies. If I stay here another minute I'll be as nuts as you are."

He rushed out the door with his empty suitcase and the box with his stuff and ran down the road to where he had left Jenny still covered with dirt. It was turning light. He opened the hood and fiddled with a few wires. Then he got into the driver's seat, inserted the key and it started right up. Sam took off up the road and never looked back.

He pulled into his garage and stepped out. Minnie his wife came out and extended her arms and hugged him tight.

"Sam I am so glad to see you. I have had an awful night. The dog threw up on the carpet, the baby cried when I didn't have a cookie for him and the toaster burned the toast. The alarm went off and the fire department showed up. All while you were living it up in the big city. By the way how was your trip?"

Sam took her in his arms and said, "You wouldn't believe it if I told you."

Miss Gabby

By
Beverly Anderson

Dear Miss Gabby,

We tried to rent a house two years ago and they wanted $3,000 before we could set foot in the door. You know, first and last and clean-up and all that. You see we had been living with my folks and it was getting a bit crowded with the six kids and all. We had to do something.

My wife saw a sign at a house that said, "Move in today, nothing down" Wow, such a deal.

Sure enough we moved into our dream home, a sweet two story with three bedrooms and two baths. Imagine! Life was darn good.

Then, guess what? I lost my job and the bank was ready to foreclose. We made plans to move back to my folks in a little trailer in their back yard. Then the government stepped in and said "Don't you dare move out. We already have too many abandoned houses. You just stay where you are and we won't charge you a penny."

Well, the wife and kids and I are happy as clams. Except now we need a car, you know to get back and forth to the grocery store and church and such. Do you think our good old government would buy us one?

Signed,
Down, but not Out (Get it?)

Dear Down,

I don't see why not. You've proven your worthiness by occupying an abandoned house. The auto manufacturers need more good American citizens just like you. Go for it!

Miss Potts and Musical Bucket

By
Beverly Anderson

"Mr. Jarvis," she said as she hurried into the boss's office, "I'm so sorry I'm late. I know you fire people who are late for work, but please don't fire me. I really need this job." Mr. Jarvis, a tall stick-like man with a heart of gold smiled at her with a twinkle in his eye and bent his chair back waiting for the story.

"Miss Potts, what crazy story do you have to tell me this time?"

Bertha Mae had been late before, but could always talk her way out of being fired. This time she had to come up with a good story, or she would be out of a job.

"I know when you hear my story—you might even give me a raise," Bertha Mae sputtered pushing her blonde curls away from her face. "You know how successful I've been in the past selling our company's new product, the musical milk buckets to the local farmers? This morning on my way to work, a cow with a very full udder stepped out in front of my car. I honked and inched forward. She wouldn't move. Finally I got out of the car and tried to chase her off the road. She still wouldn't budge an inch. I scratched my head as to what to do and it came to me she was miserable because of her full udder.

"I opened my trunk and got out the musical milk bucket, turned it on and started to milk her. Thank you for insisting your sales people always carry a milking stool along with the supply of buckets. That cow was so happy she would have followed me anywhere. People who were driving by, stopped and watched. Everyone wanted to buy one of those musical buckets. Cow's love music you know."

"I sold all twenty buckets in my trunk, and have orders for twenty more and that's why I'm late."

"Miss Potts, that's the most amazing story I've ever heard. You need to give me some time to think about this. Come back and see me this afternoon when your work is caught up. I am sure you have customers waiting."

"Oh, thank you Mr. Jarvis. I'll see you later then." She turned, gave a huge sigh, straightened her shoulders and walked out.

Much later, after packing a load of orders for musical milk buckets; Bertha Mae went over to the boss's office and knocked on the door.

"Come in."

Being careful to conduct herself with decorum she entered and sat down in a chair across from his desk. Would he fire her for what he must know was a made up story?

"Bertha Mae, with your ingenuity and spunk you certainly deserve a raise, but more importantly, you should have a new office. You have proven yourself adept and handy with the experimental musical buckets. The board and I have decided your office will move to our demonstration barn. Bus loads of kids arrive every day to see the cows milked. They will enjoy watching you milk the happy cows. Now get out of here and get to work." He laughed as he pushed her out the door.

As Bertha Mae Potts left Mr. Jarvis' office with a huge smile on her face and a light hearted skip to her feet, she thought, what a great day it was. She had managed to talk her way out of being fired again!

Millionaire

By
Beverly Anderson

Wealth, millions, ease.
Comfort, friends if you please.
Glamour, charities, parties.
Movies, stars, varieties.

Then,
Stock market blues—no job.
Bank overdraft, I sob.
When? Where?, it's gone,
Good life, my life, all done.

But wait! Faith, love, family.
Laughter, wedding, baby.
Health, hope, vision.
Money is an illusion!

Soldiers on Parade

By
Beverly Anderson

"Hey Claude, we're planning our annual Veterans Day Celebration. I know it's only May, but we need to get going on this." Claude wasn't a bit surprised to get a request from Rupert, the City Manager. They were good friends, but he wondered what he wanted now.

"Can you get your guy's down at the VFW to march in the parade? You know, wear uniforms, carry the flag, whatever. Think you can do it?"

Claude drew in his breath. "Uh, those old guys? March? You must be kidding!"

"Oh, come on. You can whip them into shape. You've got six months. We need you. Get back to me when you get organized. Okay?" Rupert hung up.

In shock, Claude grabbed his half empty coffee cup off the counter and wandered over to his recliner. He sat down and sighed. His buddies down at the VFW knew how to tell war stories; drink coffee and once a year sell poppies, but march? Nah he didn't think so.

Betty, walked into the room, collected her crocheting and sat down in the other recliner. "You look dejected. What's the matter?"

"Rupert wants us VFW guys to march in the Veterans Day Parade. Can you believe it? Us old geezers march in a parade? We're all in our seventies and Pete's over eighty. We haven't marched in fifty years. He must be joking."

"Well, that is a stretch, but I bet they can do it. I have confidence in you." Betty looked down and continued crocheting. She grinned. Those old coots march down Main Street. It was all she could do to keep a straight face.

A few days later Claude called George, the VFW Commander and told him about the City Manager's request. George was speechless.

"He wants a bunch of old guys to march in a parade? Claude, we'll look like buffoons. It'll be a disgrace to the United States Army".

"Oh come on George. It'll be good for us. Give us something new to think about. We need some excitement around the old hall. We're turning into a bunch of has-beens. I'm willing to try, but I need your support. Could you announce it at the meeting on Wednesday?" Claude surprised himself. He hadn't been this enthused about anything in years. By golly—we're going to get some life back into our meetings yet.

Okay, I'll announce it and ask the guys to get on board, but, it's your baby and if it falls apart, don't blame me. I think it's a long shot."

He hung up and went out to his immaculate garage. He'd always been neat, but during his stint in the Army his tidiness almost became an obsession. Opening the metal ladder he climbed to the attic, pushed the door aside and struggled to bring the large box to the floor. It hadn't been opened in years. Army memento's, including his uniform were inside. As he sat beside it and blew the dust from the lid, memories flooded back. Two things that were not inside were his two purple hearts which were safely framed and hung on their bedroom wall. He could almost hear Betty now when she had said. *"Let's hang these in the living room."* He didn't like to talk about the war—it's in the past and he preferred to keep it that way. If they hung in the living room, there would be questions and comments.

Claude lifted his OD dress jacket and pants and shook them. They were wrinkled and smelled of moth balls. They'd have to go to the cleaners. The ribbons were intact. He lifted the boots. An old fashioned spit shine, that's what they needed. He thought of the ship crossing the Atlantic and all the times he had polished them as he and the other troops readied for inspection.

Betty disturbed his reverie. "Lunch is ready. It's after twelve and my meeting at the church is at one. You'll have to drive me." She went back into the kitchen. Claude gathered his things and stuffed them back in the box and put the ladder away. He carried the box into the bedroom. He would deal with it later.

The day of the VFW meeting, Claude took his uniform and boots out of the closet. He glanced at the purple hearts. On the day of the parade, he'd take one out of the frame and pin it on his uniform He had gained a few pounds over the years, would he be able to get into his uniform? He slipped his arms into the jacket. It felt a little tight, but not too bad. Of course he couldn't button it, but the back could be let out. Next he picked up the pants and put them on. No surprise there, he couldn't button the fly, but the wide seam in the back could be adjusted. Everything would be taken care of by the tailor. He tried on his hat and it fit just fine. At least his head hadn't changed. Betty would probably dispute that.

The hurdle of the uniform problem had been solved, but that night he would have to do some fast talking to convince the guys to cooperate. That might take some doing, but by now he was so fired up; he hoped they would catch his enthusiasm.

Following a fine supper in their small kitchen, he gave Betty a quick kiss. "Wish me luck. I'm going to need it," he said as he went out to the garage. Earlier it occurred to him to wear his uniform to the meeting, just to help his cause, but since he wouldn't be able to button it, he figured it should be left at home.

As he walked in the door of the VFW hall, he drew in a quick breath. Commander George and nearly all of them were already there.

"Hey, Claude, I didn't see you at the pool-hall yesterday. Betty got you working in the garden?"

"Yeah, we planted a big one and the weeds seem to grow faster than the vegetables."

George cleared his throat, rapped the gavel and the meeting began. The Chaplain gave a prayer; they saluted the flag, and called the roll. New business came next.

"Claude has something to talk to you about and I want to go on record that I support him 100%. I hope you all will too."

He handed the mic to Claude. "Guys, I have an idea. Now don't decide we can't do it until you hear the whole thing." He explained that the City Manager had called and asked him if the VFW would be willing to march in the Veteran's Parade on the 11th of November.

"I was shocked at first, but the more I thought about it, the better I liked it." The fellows squirmed in their seats. Some snickered, a few whispered; but nearly everyone smiled. Tony, always against anything new, scowled.

Claude cleared his throat. "So, what do you think about the idea?"

His friend Floyd, the first to stand, said, "Hey, I think it's great. A good chance to strut our stuff and let the community see how proud we are of our service."

Tony pulled himself up. "You must be a bit addled, Claude. Do you think a bunch of weak, out of shape old guys can march three miles? What do we use for rifles—broom sticks? He smirked, and then went on, "I know damn well there's no way I can get into my uniform. It's a dumb idea. Why don't we sell pop and candy or something to support the parade? March? No way!"

A few grumbled under their breath. Another few laughed. George rapped the gavel.

"Okay, men, Claude has supported us all these years, now it's our turn to support him. I'm calling for a vote. All those in favor of marching in the parade, raise your hands. Those opposed? It's a majority, we're with you Claude. Get your plan together and let us know when the first practice is.

He took care of a few other agenda items, then George announced, "There being no further business, the meeting is adjourned."

The next day Claude drove over to the high school and caught the principal getting out of his car. "Mr. Conway, I'm Claude Johnson from the VFW. My troops and I will be marching in the Veterans Day Parade and we wonder if we could practice in the school parking lot. We'll practice Saturday mornings. Would that work?"

"I don't see why not. Our band will also be in the parade, but they practice during the week, usually on the football field. You go for it."

"Thanks so much, Mr. Conway," Claude said as he walked away with a new spring in his step. He couldn't wait to call the guys and tell them the good news.

The following Saturday, twenty five veterans showed up at the school parking lot. They all carried a long stick or a broom to simulate the rifle they would carry during the parade. One of the fellows offered to get permission from the armory to borrow rifles just prior to the parade. Claude and George stood to the side and discussed the practice session. Claude asked George to bring up the rear while he led the troops.

"Men, line up. place your toes on the crack in the pavement. Put your rifles over your right shoulder and stand up straight," Claude ordered. The men tip-toed around trying to get both feet in a straight line. They bumped each other with their fake rifles. Claude thought they looked and acted like a bunch of sheep.

"Okay, make two lines. Count off. Odd numbers fall back making a second line. Even numbers form the first line. Keep your toes on the crack in the pavement. Second line, position yourselves directly behind a man in front of you. Keep your line straight."

"Harch, one, two three," Claude yelled.

"Halt, Halt! Don't you guys remember you always start with your left foot? Tony, your other left foot. Let's try it again. Back to the crack in the pavement. Line yourselves up, now. Come on you can do this."

"Harch, left, right, left, right. Hut, two, three," Claude marched along beside them, George bringing up the rear. They were awful. They worked at it for over an hour. One dropped his broom; another slammed someone in the head.

"Okay, okay, that's enough for today," Claude said. "We'll pick it up next Saturday. They staggered back to their cars.

The next Saturday, the men were a little more enthusiastic. Everybody talked about their gear. Some had retrieved their uniforms and taken them to the cleaners for alterations and cleaning. Some had exchanged with others who had lost weight and needed a smaller uniform. Claude had made the arrangements with the armory and they would provide rifles for the parade. A spark of new life had ignited the old veterans.

*_*_*_*_*

In early October spirits began to lift. The men marched with precision, almost. Their enthusiasm matched the beauty of the fall leaves, all gold, yellow and red.

Then it happened. Betty was out for her evening walk. Claude hadn't even noticed she was gone. He was reading the latest VFW magazine. The phone rang.

"Is this Claude Johnson?"

"Uh, yes," Claude said. "Who's this?"

"This is the State Patrol. There has been an accident. Your wife was taken to the hospital in Gardner."

"Oh, no. She was just out walking. What happened?"

"They'll fill you in at the hospital. You'll want to get there as soon as you can. Do you have someone who can drive you?"

"Yeah, yeah, I'll call my son. We'll be right there" Claude hung up and dialed Don's number. No one answered. He grabbed his coat from the closet and ran to the garage. His heart and mind raced. What could have happened? Betty took her walk every evening. She never had a problem before.

Claude drove thirty miles to the hospital, parked the car and rushed through the emergency room double doors. Several patrolmen were talking to a doctor.

"I'm Claude Johnson, where's my wife?"

One of the patrolmen stepped over to him and touched his shoulder. "Let's go to the waiting room and sit down. I'll explain what happened."

"No, I want to see my wife. Where is she?"

"Calm down, you can't see her right now. She's being examined by several doctors." Claude let the patrolman lead him to the waiting room. As they sat down, he again asked what happened.

"Your wife was at the crosswalk on Highway 64. The driver in the lane next to her stopped and waved her on. A driver in the inside lane didn't see her as she stepped in front of him."

"Oh, God, no, no," Claude sobbed and held his head.

"Both drivers were devastated. She's in intensive care. The doctor said they'll be taking her into surgery soon. I'm sorry, sir." The patrolman left as a nurse entered the room.

"You can go see your wife for a few minutes before they take her to surgery."

Claude jumped up and followed the nurse down the hall. He couldn't keep the tears from his eyes. They'd been married for more than forty years. He couldn't live without his Betty. As he entered her room his legs buckled. The damage done to his lovely wife was incomprehensible. The nurse helped him to a chair by her bed. A doctor and several nurses rushed into the room and he was told he should go to the waiting room where they would notify him when the surgery was over. He stood and kissed Betty's hand, the only part of her that wasn't covered in blood and tubes.

After returning to the waiting room Claude called his son, Don. This time he answered. "Don, this is dad. Your mom has been in an accident. She's in surgery at Sacred Heart. Call your brother and you two get down here. I need you and so does mom. It wasn't long before the boys and their wives showed up at the hospital. The vigil began. Several hours went by. They all paced the floor, going for coffee at the cafeteria now and then. Food was not needed or wanted.

Finally the doctor came into the waiting room. "Your wife will recover, but it's going to be a long, hard struggle. I can't assure you that she will be her old self. Time will tell. She has been severely injured. We'll move her to a larger hospital, where they have better and more modern equipment.

"When will she have to be moved?" Claude asked.

"She's in a coma and we won't move her for at least a week. You can go in to see her, but you should go home and get some rest. It's going to be a long haul." The doctor left.

Indeed it was. Eventually, they took Betty in an ambulance to the regional hospital. She had been in a coma for over ten days and several times they thought she was near death. Claude sat by her bedside, only leaving now and then to get something to eat. After two weeks, she opened her eyes and spoke a few garbled words, but it was a month before she recognized Claude and the family. The long drive to the large regional hospital each week took planning and schedule changes. Their dad would be forever thankful, for his son's and their wives who never failed to take turns at her bedside.

Claude hadn't had much time to think about the parade, but George called soon after the accident and assured him they would keep practicing. Tony even offered to be the liaison between the men and their leader. He and Frank sent flowers to Betty and several times took homemade soup, bread and cookies to Claude's house. They called frequently to see if there was anything they could do. Claude, comforted by the care they showed, but he had lost his appetite and had also lost weight. One night he realized he shouldn't have had his uniform altered. Would it hang loosely on him now?

The first of November arrived and the men were getting excited about the parade. Claude made the one hundred mile trip to the hospital each week and spent nights with friends who lived near the hospital. He came home on Friday nights, in time for practice on Saturday and church on Sunday. On Mondays he drove back to the hospital.

Finally, they got the good news. She had made enough progress and she could go home. A nurse would be needed during the day, but Claude would take care of her at night. He hired Andrea a local nurse's aide.

The morning of November 11th, Claude couldn't sleep. He turned everything over and over in his mind, but mostly it was the parade. Padding in pajamas and slippers to the kitchen, he poured a cup of coffee from the automatic pot he always set the night before. Would the guys be able to march the three miles through town? Would they keep cadence or would they march any better than they did the first day of practice? He shook his head. Whatever. It was too late to worry about it now. He marveled at the beautiful sun peeking over the horizon in the east. The week before had been rainy and overcast. It was a good omen.

Betty must be awake by now, so he fixed her breakfast tray as he did each morning. It was a pleasure to have his dear wife home with him, even though she wasn't the same and maybe never would be. He was thankful for what they had.

Claude dressed in his cleaned and pressed uniform. He pinned his Purple Heart on his jacket and looked in the mirror. He didn't look too bad, despite the heartache he had been through. As he walked into the living room where Betty sat with the nurse, she mumbled something.

"What is it?' he asked as he sat down beside her. She patted his purple heart and with the look in her eyes, he knew she wanted to tell him how good he looked. He kissed her on the cheek.

"Come on honey. We're going to take you down to main-street so you and Andrea can watch the parade. I'll get a blanket for you and you'll be nice and warm in the car." Claude got a blanket out of the closet and Andrea helped Betty into her wheel chair.

People of every age lined the streets and looked expectantly toward the West end of town where the parade would begin right on time. The local high school band led the parade, playing patriotic songs. The mayor and his wife followed in a bright red 1968 Mustang. Several bands came from neighboring towns and the kids marched in precision as young people are able to do. Music wafted through the air and lifted people's spirits. Flowery floats from local towns and communities, riders on horseback and clowns throwing candy to the kids delighted everyone. Finally, the VFW took their place in the parade. Claude called cadence as they marched down the street. Their uniforms, altered and cleaned, looked sharp and if you didn't look too close they could almost pass for young, able-bodied men. Their faces showed grim determination, as they marched by with nearly perfect timing, rifles perched on their shoulders. Two ROTC students carried flags. People removed their hats and held their hands over their hearts.

They did it. Meetings at the VFW Hall would not be as dull as they had been in the past. These old guys felt they could do anything they set their minds to and who knew what their next assignment might be. They had overcome their doubts and mastered their assignment.

Claude, Betty and Andrea went home, happy and thankful. Life, returning to normal, would never be quite the same, but they could deal with it.

Claude decided the VFW should have a party and they would invite Rupert the City Manager. If it hadn't been for him, the VFW probably would have been like the saying:

"Old Soldiers Never Die, They Just Fade Away."

The Outhouse

By
Beverly Anderson

Cold in winter, hard, rough pine seat.
On the door a half moon, ambiance replete.
Melodorous, stinky, reeking, smells.
Over time the disgusting waste swells.

Too far from the house, through the snow, an approach.
Disgusting inhabitants, flies, bees and a roach.
Too close to the house, odor wafts through the air.
Halloween, they tip it, the cover is bare.

Miss the cold outhouse? No not one iota.
Especially the ones in old North Dakota.

Cinquain Poem

By
Beverly Anderson

Overeating
Whole Pie
Consumed, Devoured, Gobbled
Stuffed, Bloated, Ballooned, Enlarged
Disgusting

Adventure on the Dolomites

By
Beverly Anderson

Anthony Genaro looked out of his second story window. It's snowing on the Dolomites and it's only September, he thought. In every one of Tony's nineteen years he dreamed of hiking those Italian Alps. They fascinated him. He packed his gear and wondered if the snow would hinder that dream.

"Anthony, Anthony, if you don't hurry you'll miss your breakfast."

"Yeah, mama, I'm on my way." Tony grabbed his pack, hiking shoes, sun glasses and hat and took the stairs missing at least half of them. Mama and Papa sat at the kitchen table finishing the hearty breakfast they enjoyed every morning.

"Rosa, you are such a good mama. You feed your boy, then send him off to kill himself on those old mountains."

"Hush, Pasquali—you're just jealous. You know you want to go too, but your son must go alone to prove himself. Now eat your sausages, and be quiet."

Tony slid onto his chair at the table. He ate his sausages, tomatoes and cheese between gulps of coffee while his parents discussed their activities for the coming day. Tony glanced at the window. The sun shone and he gazed out at the Alps as he had done nearly every day of his life. He was glad his mama believed in a good breakfast. He would need it for the climb, but planned to be back home by supper time. In the future he would climb higher and longer, but for the first time, it would be a day hike.

He gathered his things and headed for the door, but couldn't leave until his mama had demanded kisses and his papa hugs. The bus brakes squealed as it pulled to a stop on the street below. Tony ran out and waved to the driver.

"Good Morning Tony my boy. Where are you off to this time?" Guiseppe asked.

"I'm going to hike the trail up the Dolomites." as Tony grabbed the bar and swung into the seat closest to the front.

"I hope you have a map and a warm coat. I see it's snowing on the peaks."

Tony settled into his seat and took out his map. The bus went as far as the beginning of the trail. After a year of planning this adventure, the time had come. School was over and his summer job finished. A bit of snow wouldn't stop him.

Finally the bus pulled into the trailhead and Tony was the only passenger left.

"Good luck, Mr. Tony."

"Thanks! I'll be fine I'm sure."

The trail was well groomed and led off through the rocks and trees. Tony adjusted his pack, put on his hat and sunglasses and started off up the trail. Thinking he felt good didn't describe his complete euphoria. As a young child he had asked his dad if he could climb the Dolomites and his dad laughed at his innocence. "Some day, son. Some day." That *some day* was finally here.

As Tony walked, the alpine smells, subtle breezes, and sound of his shoes touching the rocky surfaces heightened all his senses. Climbing higher and higher the trail steepened. He noticed some movement across the ravine. He had seen no other hiker on the trail in the last two hours so the movement startled him. To his surprise a band of black mountain sheep moved across the white snow field. There were so many. Awesome.

After awhile he came to a place to take a lunch break and sat down by a huge boulder. Dropping his pack he retrieved a bottle of water. He was thirstier than he realized and after a long drink, hunger pangs assaulted him. In his lunch bag; there were three meatball sandwiches. He kissed his fingertips and saluted his good Italian mama.

Tony sat on the rock and munched. He looked down the trail toward what sounded like voices. Someone must be coming he thought. The voices got louder and as they rounded the corner he could see it was a young couple loaded with gear. The girl was limping and the boy was tramping ahead unaware or uncaring, Tony wasn't sure.

"Hey, we're going to the top, want to come along?" the boy asked when he saw Tony.

"I guess not, I'm not geared for an overnight. Just doing a day hike. My name's Tony. Nice to meet you."

"Yeah, I'm Aldo and this is Branca. Hurry up. She's so slow."

"My ankle hurts, Aldo. Can't we just sit here for awhile?"

"OK, OK, just sit."

Tony moved over. He felt sorry for the young girl who seemed to be in real pain. "What happened to your ankle?" he asked.

"Oh, I was trying to catch up back on the trail and I slipped off the edge. Alda tied a rope around his waist and threw the other end to me. I was able to pull myself up. I thought I could keep walking, but it's starting to hurt worse."

"I don't think you should go any further," Tony said. "It may be badly sprained."

"Hey fellow, stay out of this. She's just fine and we're going to the top. A little sprain ain't goin' to stop us. Come on Branca."

"Aldo, I can't. See how swollen it is? It hurts too bad. You go on. I'll rest awhile and then start down."

"Oh, sure, wimp out on me. I should have known better than take a silly girl on a mountain climbing trip. Go on back to your mama. Next time I'll ask Frederica."

Aldo stomped off up the trail, leaving Branca in tears and Tony feeling helpless.

"Would you like a drink of water?" he asked. "I also have an extra sandwich, you're welcome to it."

They both sat beside the rock. Branca didn't move. The silent tears spilled onto her jacket.

"I know I shouldn't have come with Aldo. He made it sound so exciting and I knew if I didn't go with him he wouldn't have any trouble finding someone else. My mama warned me."

Tony took her ankle in his hands and felt the severe swelling. He pulled her boot off.

"Oooh, that hurts."

"I'm sorry, but this needs to be wrapped and there's no way you can walk down the mountain. I have an elastic bandage in my pack. Let me wrap it for you."

After Tony wrapped Branca's ankle, he helped her to her feet. He put his arm around her back and slung her pack on top of his own. They started down the trail. The sun was beginning to set in the West casting shadows on the rocks they struggled to negotiate. Hours passed. They rested at every turn and Tony adjusted the packs. Tony was happy he could help this young girl, but once in awhile he gazed back at the peaks. Maybe I'm not meant to hike the Dolomites he thought. Papa was right. He always refused to talk about them or even consider taking his young son up there.

It was dark when they reached the bus stop. They waited. The last bus pulled up to the trail head. The door swung open.

"Mr. Tony, where'd you get this pretty girl? You didn't tell me you went hunting."

"We're so glad to see you Pasquali. We had a little trouble on the trail and Branca hurt her ankle. She'll be OK as soon as she gets some rest." Tony helped her onto the bus. He tossed the packs onto the adjacent seat. The bus bounced down the hill and Tony and Branca fell back in exhaustion. Lulled by the rhythm of the bus bumping over the rough, pot hole riddled road they immediately fell asleep.

"Wake up Tony, here's your stop." The bus driver pulled over to the side of the road and opened the door. Branca jerked awake and sat up.

"I must get off here Branca. Where do you live? Maybe papa can drive you there."

"Oh, no. I'll find another bus. I live many miles from here. Aldo and I hitched a ride to get to the Dolomites."

"No Branca, you are in no condition to walk anywhere. Come home with me. My mama will feed us—then we can talk about how you will get home."

Tony could tell Branca was in too much pain and too tired to argue. He helped her up the steep, winding path to his home. His mama heard them coming and called to him as he opened the door.

"Tony is that you?" He could never sneak home late because of that squeaky door his papa refused to fix. On second thought, maybe his mama didn't want it fixed.

'Yes, and I've brought someone with me."

His mama came out of the bedroom. Papa followed as they adjusted their robes and tried to open their eyes.

"Who have you brought and why are you so late? Your mama and I have been worried."

"This is Branca. She sprained her ankle on the trail. She should see a doctor, but it'll have to wait until morning. Is there any food left from supper? We are so hungry."

Mama scurried to the kitchen. "Come, come. I have plenty left. I always save for you Tony-you know that. Branca you come too. You must be starved."

Papa trailed along and they all sat down at the homey kitchen table with the red checked cloth. Tony and Branca dug into the pasta, tomato salad with goat cheese and garlic olive bread as if they hadn't eaten in weeks. Papa peppered them with questions.

"Where do you come from Branca? Were you climbing in the Dolomites alone?"

"Oh, no. I'd be too afraid." Branca swallowed and went on. "My papa died up there before I was born. Mama didn't want mc to go, but Aldo insisted. Aldo is my boyfriend. Well he was . . ."

"Papa, Aldo wanted Branca to keep going even after she hurt her ankle. I offered to stay with her and help her off the mountain."

"Branca, you say your papa died on the mountain? What was your papa's name?" Pasquali asked with tremor in his voice. Rosa stared at the young girl. Could it be? She was the right age.

"My Papa's name was Vincent Scallici Genaro. Why do you ask?"

"Oh Mama, Mama . . . after all these years."

Tony's papa rose from his seat and walked over to Branca. He put his hands on her shoulders.

"Vincent, was my brother. We had a quarrel after our papa died. He said he never wanted to see me again. He moved away. We heard he married and had a child. You must be that child, Branca. Bellissimo, Bellissimo. Praise, Mother of God."

"But how did you know how he died?"

"We heard through friends. After he died we tried to find you and your mama, but you had moved away."

"Tony, you brought your cousin home to us-my brother's daughter. She must stay the night. Tomorrow we will take her home to her mama."

After Branca was settled into the guest room, Tony climbed the stairs to his room. What a day he thought. Now I know why papa would never take me to the mountains. No wonder he was against my going. His brother died up there. If I had not gone, we may never have found Branca and her mama.

Life is full of surprises he thought and I'm sure there will be many more before I leave this earth.

Margaret's Stories

Margaret Watland

Margaret Watland hails from a small farming community in southeast Washington. As a child, Margaret was always being told to stop daydreaming. She was in her forties before realizing her daydreams were stories waiting to be written.

Margaret has written church newsletters and bulletins. During the last three years of her banking career, Margaret wrote procedures and performance reviews for her 29 employees. She has taken creative writing and related classes at two community colleges. She has attended writer's conferences both in Washington and Arizona. She been active in several different writers groups and has presented her work at public readings.

She is seventy-four years old and writes. Margaret has completed a series of children's stories about the nativity as seen through the eyes of two young children.

She gathers family stories for her grandchildren and plans to put them in book form.

RECALLING MY WWII EXPERIENCES

By
Virgil Watland and Margaret Watland

My name is Virgil Watland I was born May 30, 1923. I am a veteran of World War II.

I want to share with you some of my experiences while serving on the battleship USS Colorado. I am 81 years old so I have had to use books written by other shipmates to spark my memory. I am being as honest as possible but there are a few occasions where I disagree with my other shipmates. I am telling my story the way I remember it.

Chapter One

I was 17 when I graduated from high school in Armstrong, Iowa. I wanted to join the Navy but promised my Uncle Allie I'd stay around until the corn was picked. November 28, 1941, I went to Minneapolis and joined the Navy.

I was sent to The Great Lakes Training Center in Illinois. Nine days later the Japanese attacked Pearl Harbor. I don't think there was anybody in my company who knew where Pearl Harbor was located. While I was at the training center I had all my hair cut off, learned how to tie a square knot and a bowline knot, and received numerous shots.

Learning to sleep in a hammock wasn't easy. They taught us to string up a hammock about three and one-half feet above the deck. It took a few tries to maneuver getting into the *hammock,* navy lingo! About the time we'd get to sleep somebody would fall out. This happened quite frequently the first few nights. I slept in a hammock my first two and a half years in the Navy. I should have been in boot camp for three months, but instead I was aboard ship in less than a month.

On Christmas Eve, we were on a train speeding towards the Puget Sound. We were served a wonderful dinner. The next morning the conductor pointed out Mt. Rainier and soon afterward, we arrived in Seattle, Washington. We were taken to Bremerton on the ferry Kalakala. There were times on the ferry ride to Bremerton when it was a long way from land. This Iowa farm boy got nervous on that trip because I wasn't that great a swimmer. It was then I wondered if I had made the right choice in joining the Navy.

When we arrived in Bremerton, they took us first to the YMCA for a medical check and then on to the battleship USS Colorado which was in the shipyard for overhaul. They lined us up on the quarterdeck and asked if we wanted to go below decks or up on the guns. If I'd been smart, I would have chosen to go below decks. I might have learned a trade but being young I, and a lot of the others said, "The guns!"

I was assigned to the 6A Division, which manned the 5"/ 25 caliber anti-aircraft guns. That was my battle station throughout the war. My first meal aboard the Colorado was Christmas dinner. It was delicious!

Beginning in early summer, after the ship's overhaul was completed, we patrolled up and down the West Coast.

In August, we were sent to Pearl Harbor. Evidence of the December 7th bombing was everywhere. While we were standing watch, our shipmate Hood stood on the gun shield and stared and stared at the capsized battleship USS Utah that was berthed directly behind us. His brother lay immersed in the water aboard that ship.

Word came that the Japanese were trying to fortify the Aleutian Islands. We already knew there were Japanese on the Islands. The Colorado and several other ships were sent there to intercept. One of our patrol planes from the battleship USS New Mexico came flying in low through a heavy fog trying to locate his ship. The end of the plane's wing tip hit us up on the mast. The plane twirled a couple of times, and landed upside down in the water. We stopped and lowered our sailors into a motor whaleboat to try a rescue. They attached a line to the plane and brought it back alongside our ship. When a boom lifted the plane aboard, the dead pilot fell out on the quarterdeck. We never found the radioman.

October 1942, the Colorado and some of the other repaired ships from the Pearl Harbor attack were sent down to the Fiji Islands There was concern that the Japanese might try to take New Zealand. We were sent there to be back up. On one of our liberties we went ashore and walked to a little town on the island of Viti Levu. It looked like a little western town with wooden sidewalks. We saw pineapple plantations off in the distance. The people were large and the men had big bushy hair.

We went back and forth between the Fiji Islands and the New Hebrides. We walked to a little village nearby that was quite primitive. One hut had a door on all four sides. As we walked around the hut the naked children inside would run from door to door to stare at us. We built our own recreation center on the New Hebrides. We were there on Christmas of 1942. A small USO troop came through and introduced us to a new Christmas song that was popular back in the states, "White Christmas."

A year later in October 1943 we were back in Pearl Harbor. By this time those in authority thought we had enough ships to start "taking back" some of the allied islands that the Japanese held. Our first Island "take back" was in the Marshall Islands at Tarawa. November 20 we began several days of bombardment on Tarawa. The Japs had made some strong pillboxes (fortified concrete gun emplacements with a low flat roof).

They also used heavy timbers and bulldozed a lot of sand on top to strengthen them. The leaves of the palm trees were shredded. Devastation was everywhere. When the Marines went ashore, it was nip and tuck for a while. This was how they finally took Tarawa.

One of our destroyers "depth charged" a Japanese submarine. It was forced to come up to the surface. Another of our destroyers rammed the sub. A pilot from the Colorado landed and tried to pick up one of the Jap survivors. The pilot had to shoot the Jap when he tried to punch a hole in the plane's pontoon. Slowly the sub tipped vertically and was silhouetted against the red glow of the sunset as it sank into the deep.

At the completion of that campaign our ship finally returned to Bremerton. I got my boot leave after two and a half years in the Navy.

Nature's Musical

By
Margaret Watland

"**OOOEEE**—OO—oo—oo," coos the pigeon in a low voice
A chorus sings forth with cheeps, chips, and chitters.
At dawn a full voiced choir lures me outside.
My lounger faces riverside. The morning sun warms my back.

O Lord, this is so glorious!
"**OOOEEE**—OO—oo—oo," echoes high in the trees.
Scores of sparrows swoop to and fro.
One calmly sits bobbing on a wire thin branch.

A robin tugs a worm from the ground,
stands to contemplate, then flies away.
The robin's orange flashes through the tapestry
of the bright green sugar maple leaves.

A fresh breeze tempers the rising heat.
My Bible's pages flutter. Concentration departs.
I've lost my place. My coffee's cold.
"**OOOEEE**—OO—oo—oo," soothes my soul.

Strolling along a row of thistle are two quail,
topknots ruffling, heads flipping back and forth.
She's so plain but he's dressed for morning calls.
They appear to be so fearful. Can't they see me?

Pirouetting over a thistle bloom,
a tiny goldfinch feasts on the plentiful seeds.
Her unfurled wings reveal pale yellows and greens
as she hovers, feeding to her fill.

I sit immobile, admiring these birds of the air,
knowing the slightest movement could frighten them.
A whiff of mock orange floats by on the breeze.
The sun climbs higher into a deep blue sky.

The music changes. It's a fast boogie.
Different voices join the singing
but the pigeon stays, maintaining his tempo,
with a gentle haunting "**OOOEEE**—OO—oo - oo."

My Family Recipe

By
Margaret Watland

Have you ever wondered if you had an Al Capone, a Jesse James, or royal blood in your background? My Dad used to wonder if my mother had blue blood in her veins. I thought his reasoning on the subject was ridiculous so we won't go into that.

One day about a year after my mother's death I received an invitation to the Adams' family reunion. Adams was my mother's maiden name. Her father died when she was five and I knew very little about that side of her family.

I remember her talking about a cousin from her father's side. Mother told us about having seen this cousin, Elizabeth, a couple of times when they were young girls. She was sickly. She had diabetes, which had been discovered when she was a baby. The shocking thing about her was she married a Japanese minister. Mother's story was that a lot of the family disowned her. Mother knew Elizabeth had children—half white, half Japanese!

The reunion was being held in Sequim. My husband Victor was willing to go with me so I sent off money for the dinner and put together a little book of old photos of Mother and some of our family. I was hoping I would hear stories about mother when she was a little girl. I looked forward to sharing things about her and our family. I had an exit speech ready if we found the Adams family reunion too boring to tolerate.

We arrived at the Lodge listed on the invitation and timidly walked in. Stella the organizer of the reunion immediately spotted us and made us feel comfortable. She introduced us to her elderly father George and suggested we sit down at their table. Stella sat at the end of the table with her computer. We quickly discovered they were into genealogy and Stella wanted names and addresses to add to their chart. Later Stella's father showed us his family chart, which was very impressive. It went back to before the Revolutionary War. It was fascinating listening to his stories!

People stopped by to meet us and I showed them my little photo album. A few cousins told me stories about mother and showed me pictures of their family. I heard different ones saying the twins were coming. Stella told me the twins were Elizabeth's children. Stella said the twins were adopted. Elizabeth and her husband chose to adopt babies who were of mixed race—Japanese and Caucasian.

It was obvious the family loved those twins. We were just about to sit down to dinner when they arrived. In walked two tall, slim, dark haired young men. Happy greetings came forth from the crowd. I didn't see their Japanese side in their faces.

Stella's father suggested we stop by his house before we went home. He wanted to show us some interesting old letters.

George was in his glory talking about our ancestors. I learned they could not find an Adams name on any of the ships that landed on American shores. Servants and prisoners names were not listed on the ship's logs in those days so we don't know our nationality!

When we arrived at George's home he pointed us to a comfortable couch, excused himself and slipped away to a back room. He returned with a handful of old papers, and then began telling us what Mother would have called "the dirt" about our family. He showed us a letter written by an Aunt Hettie that described a trip she and her husband Uncle Ralph had taken during the prohibition era. The letter was written to a girl friend. Aunt Hettie wrote that they drove by the light of the moon down back farm roads. Car lights appeared in the distance so they turned their car onto Cousin Herman's field and bumped across the rough ground, crossed a creek, and eventually connected with another road that took them to the city. Aunt Hettie said they got to their destination without breaking any of the carefully wrapped mason jars George saved the best for last. He pulled a ragged yellowed piece of paper out from among his papers and handed it to me. "Here is a recipe you might want to copy," he said with a smile and a twinkle in his eye.

I must share my recipe with you!

Recipe for Moonshine

50 pounds of cornmeal
200 pounds of sugar
200 gallons of water
1½ cups of yeast

Don't buy your sugar all in one place because it is a sure sign to the revenuers that you are going to make moonshine.

Jelly the Teddy Bear Fairy

By
Margaret Watland

Granny Button entered the kitchen with her arms full of groceries. She heard a voice coming from the back of the house. "Oh dear, I thought I turned off the TV," she said dropping her groceries on the counter and marching down the hall to the den. Granny looked at a black TV screen.

The voice came again saying, "Hey, HEY! Come in here, Granny Button. I've been sitting on this guest bed forever. I'm so glad you finally came home! Please put me back where I belong."

Granny crept down the hall to her office with trembling hands. She reached for Jelly, her teddy bear fairy charm that hung on a gold chain around her neck. The charm was warm, almost hot and it seemed to be crawling up her finger. The teddy bear fairy charm jumped off her finger and fluttered down to stand in the middle of Granny's hand. The white-haired woman stood frozen staring down at the little gold fairy charm in her hand.

"Mrs. Button, Herman wants to go back to his family that lives under the old sewing machine. You two have thirty minutes to talk. That's all the time I can spare," said Jelly and then she disappeared.

Herman glared up at the old woman standing in front of him and said, "This bed is for company and I don't hear any company out there. I don't mind cuddling with your company. I was happy to cuddle with your tired three-year-old great-grandson Seth, but that was six weeks ago. I have been here since before Christmas. My family had to celebrate Christmas without me," said Herman. "You come in here every day and study at that messy table and work on your computer, but you never think about me."

Granny couldn't believe her ears. Herman, her big fluffy blonde teddy bear was talking to her and he was mad!

"You have a family?" she asked.

"Of course I do," said Herman. "I've adopted every one of those bears you put under the sewing machine with me. The hardest one you gave me was CNN. Did you know his legs don't move? All that little bear can do is sit. He cried and cried when he first came. I heard you tell your friend that you had given CNN to your Dad. You brought him to me after your father died."

"You named him CNN?" asked Granny.

"That was the only word he knew so that's what we called him."

"Well, that makes sense. My Dad watched CNN all day. I kept telling Dad news was depressing and he didn't need to listen to it all day," said Granny. "Does CNN still cry a lot?"

"Oh no, he has a happy loving family. CNN can't go out and play so he's our newsman. I must tell you we got mighty tired of hearing about all those Christmas love stories you watched on that Hallmark channel. Why don't you ever watch cartoons? We'd all like to see some cartoons."

"Herman, do all your bears have names? You are the only bear I've ever named."

"Of course they do but you wouldn't know how to pronounce them. They are bear names and you don't know bear language."

"I can't believe I'm talking to a teddy bear and a teddy bear fairy," said Granny as she carried Herman back to his family under the sewing machine. "This must be a dream."

"Grrr gr gr grrrowl!" Herman's return to his family caused a terrible commotion. Herman quieted each of his children with a kiss and a hug then said, "I need to talk to Granny Button right now. We'll talk later."

Herman turned to the old woman and said, "No, it's not a dream. Your fairy's name is Jjelemnzxy. You can't pronounce her name. It is a bear name."

Granny stared at Herman wide-eyed and said, "No, I can't say that. Could I call her Jelly the Teddy Bear Fairy?"

"Sure," said Herman. "Now we need to get busy and give all these children a people name. We don't have much time."

"All right let's do it," she said and picked up the next biggest bear with soft red curly fur. "This is Natalie, and next is Scruffy with his light tangled fur. Oh dear, aren't these the cutest bears. This little one is Nutmeg for the color of her fur. Herman, is this a boy or a girl?"

"The last two are boys," said Herman. "Please hurry."

"The brown bear with the white nose will be Mert, and the littlest one has fur the color of vanilla pudding. I'll call him Vanilla.

Herman looked at Granny and asked, "Mert?"

Grammy looked down and said kind of quiet like. "Well, his fur is the color of dirt but I just couldn't call him Dirt. Granny checked her watch and asked, "Will I be able to talk to you again?"

"You can talk to us any time and we'll hear you but we can't talk back to you without Jelly's help. Whenever you touch Jelly the Teddy Bear Fairy charm and it is warm, quickly put the necklace around your neck and she'll grant you some of her time. I would be very surprised if we ever talk again. She is much too busy."

"Is there anything I can do for you?" asked Granny.

"Yes please," said Herman. "Scruffy and I have satin bow ties that are kind of ragged. Natalie's bow is very nice, but CNN, Mert, Nutmeg and Vanilla are out in front of everyone without clothes. They need bow ties. Another thing—it gets dirty under the sewing machine. We could all use a special teddy bear ba . . ."

Granny felt a chill on her neck. She lifted the charm. It was cold. "Oh dear", said Granny. "My appointment is over. I have things I have to do for all my bears. I think they would like to have an outing. I'm going to take them all to Wal-Mart and we'll choose ribbon for bow ties. I need to look on the internet to get instructions on how to clean teddy bears. Nutmeg is the only one that can be washed in the washing machine."

Granny was sooo happy. She lived all by herself in her house. Now she had seven teddy bears she could talk to.

From that day on Granny always wore her necklace with the teddy bear fairy called Jelly.

Where Am I?

By
Margaret Watland

Marty rushed into her apartment, tore off her waitress uniform and dropped it onto the bed. She opened the closet door and grabbed jogging clothes. It took minutes to slip into pants, tee shirt, hoodie and running shoes. She had just opened the fridge when there was a knock at the door.

"Coming," she called as she grabbed a bottle of water and her box cutter weapon that lay on top of the 'frig. "Hi Josh. I just got home. Can we stretch at the park?"

"Sure. I almost had to call and say I couldn't make it. You remember what I told you. No jogging without me! Together we are armed enough for an evening jog. We'll have to stay on the sidewalks tonight it's getting dark too fast to run through the park," said Josh.

Marty looked up at her tall muscular neighbor. "Nag, nag! I know, I know! Are you still having problems explaining to Jimmy that anger doesn't go with karate?" she asked as they finished their stretching and started their run around the park.

"Yeah. He thinks if he gets a black belt he can win the war against gangs. I'm not going to teach a hotheaded kid that wants to pick a fight with his karate. I know his best friend was killed in a gang war. I don't teach war. I teach self defense!"

Ahead a few mature fir trees encroached the sidewalk and blocked the next streetlight. A broken limb lay across the cement. Marty tripped but caught her balance and leapt over the branch. She stopped and kicked the limb off the walkway. There was a shushing sound in the trees, Josh choking, and a loud thud. Marty whipped around with her X-acto knife open and sliced it across a stranger's Adam's apple. The man slumped to the ground with blood gushing from his neck

Josh's body lay in a misshapen pile, head twisted, eyes in a frozen stare, chin caught over his left shoulder, and blood seeping out of his facial orifices. The attacker's clothing was saturated with his own blood.

Blood dripped down from her hands. She wiped them on her pants and glanced around. It was night so the darkness hid the splatters of blood that soaked her clothing. Marty shivered and was shocked that she had survived and her friend Josh was dead.

She needed to get Josh's phone out of his pocket. Marty, a recovered alcoholic, didn't have a good reputation at police headquarters. Running was out of the question she must call 911.

"My friend was murdered and I killed the guy," she said in a low monotone.

"I don't know where I am. I'm by some big fir trees. The branches go over the sidewalk.

I'm at a, . . . a park close to my apartment. Please come quick. I think I'm going to be sick.

"Okay, I won't put the phone down. I can't remember his phone number it's on my speed dial and my phone is at home.

"The name of the park? . . . I can't remember. My name? . . . my name is Marty. My full name? . . . my full name is Martha Eloise Henderson but nobody calls me that. I'm just Marty.

"Okay, I'll sit down on the grass. Will you come soon? I'm awful cold."

While Shepherds Watched Their Flocks

By
Margaret Watland

Six-year-old Caleb, the shepherd boy, watched his three little orphaned lambs—Woolie, Sneaky, and Jumpy—playing one last game of "leap lamb" before snuggling down for the night.

Caleb tipped his face heavenward. His eyes searched the evening sky for the first star of the night. Was that a new star in the sky? It was bigger and brighter than any star Caleb had ever seen! It appeared to be right over the little town of Bethlehem. Caleb turned to tell Grandfather about the star when lightning flashed across the darkness. No, it wasn't lightning! There was no storm—no thunder—no rain—just light! The fields were filled with light—light as bright as the summer sun. The shepherds, and even the animals, stared up at the bright sky. The light was so bright that everyone held their arms up to cover their eyes. The sheep stood stiff legged—quivering in fear—making mewing sounds in their throats.

Sneaky made a whimpering bleat and he and the other two lambs crowded against Caleb. In great fright they pushed and pushed until they and Caleb were all in a tumble on the ground. Four pairs of eyes peered out and around the lambs' woolly bodies.

"Oh! Oh! Oh!" Caleb whispered. His black eyes searched for Grandfather and cousin Matthew. Matthew was thirteen and like a big brother to Caleb, they loved each other very much.

Grandfather stood like a statue listening to a voice. The light was so bright it was hard to see, but Caleb could make out the shape of a person. The bright glow around it made everything look blurry. Caleb blinked his eyes but it was still hard to see. Could it be an angel?

SILENCE! Not a sound could be heard. No bleating of the sheep, no cry, no "oah oah" of the owl, no shepherds calling quietly to one another, and no desert mice rattling the dry leaves. The bright new star was lighting all of Bethlehem.

Everything came back to life at once. Frightened sheep cried and crashed into each other, excited men shouted, and lambs bleated for their mothers. The sheep ran every direction, trying to run away from their fright.

Caleb feared they would run blindly on top of each other and hurt or even kill those underneath. The shepherds knew they must quiet the animals and help them forget their fear.

Matthew called through the noise to Caleb, "Help me pull these sheep out of the bushes. They're all tangled up!"

Matthew and Caleb pulled and tugged, ripped and tore the bucking lambs from the prickly brush." *BAA Baa Baaa*," cried one lamb right in his ear. "Ow, that hurts," Caleb hollered. The lamb quivered in fright. "Oops, I'm sorry little lamb," he whispered in the lamb's pink ear. "I made you more scared with my loud voice. Here, little fella, let me hug you right up against me so you will feel safer. I just wanted to get you unstuck. Shhh, little guy, shhh!"

Finally it looked like all the sheep were gathered together. Grandfather counted the sheep. There was one missing, a lamb.

"Oh no! Where's Sneaky? It's Sneaky! That's who's missing!" said Caleb. He ran to the nearest bushes that lined a ditch and poked his staff between the branches feeling for the soft woolly lamb.

If Sneaky wasn't stuck in those bushes, where could he be? There was a row of bushes that grew across the edge of a ridge at the top of the hill with a deep drop over a rocky cliff.

Caleb hollered back to the others, "He might be up on the hill!'

"Wait for me," called Matthew.

Caleb didn't listen, he ran up the hill as fast as he could. Breathing hard and with a pain in his side, Caleb reached the top. He crashed through the bushes catching his clothes on the thorns. He heard Sneaky's cry and stretched to see over the front branches. The lamb's head and two front legs were stuck in the bushes. His two back legs scissor kicked in the air over the rocky cliff. Caleb wrapped his arms tight around Sneaky's neck and held on with all his might.

Matthew, coming to help, followed Caleb into the bushes. Matthew's longer arms reached through the thorny branches grabbing Sneaky around the middle and both boys pulled the little lamb right through the middle of prickly limbs. Caleb fell backward with Sneaky bringing Matthew down with them into a mountainous heap.

Matthew carefully ran his hands over the trembling bleating lamb checking for anything that might be cut or broken. Caleb pulled away a sharp dead branch and discovered blood running down the inside of his arm. His scratched face and arms were smeared with blood and dirt. His tunic was torn, and sprinkled with dirt and dead leaves.

"The lamb is OK," said Matthew, "but I can't say the same for you. Don't you EVER do that again! When I tell you to wait, you wait! You and Sneaky could have fallen over that cliff. Do you hear me Caleb?"

Caleb nodded with his head down. He knew he had done wrong.

"We better get back and fix your arm!" Said Matthew as he lifted Sneaky across his shoulders. "Hold your arm up so it won't bleed so much."

Caleb sat beside the campfire while Matthew cleaned away the dirt. He wrapped a clean rag firmly around Caleb's arm. Caleb gritted his teeth and worked hard to keep the tears away. Behind him were trampled bushes with clumps of wool hanging from them. Sheep moved about in the field with dirt and bits of dry twigs stuck to their matted wool.

"That's a deep cut," said Matthew, "You'll probably have a scar on that arm. Be sure to keep it clean!"

"I will! Thank you for helping me with Sneaky."

"I'm always here to help you," said Matthew. "Are you going to wait for me next time?"

Caleb nodded yes. "I was kind of scared. I'm sorry I didn't obey you."

Matthew picked up his flute. "Good! Now it's time I played some music to help calm these sheep," he said.

Matthew's flute music swirled around the animals and finally they began to lie down. The music lulled them to sleep.

Grandfather, Uncle Reuben (Matthew's father), and Uncle Ben gathered together at the campfire. Matthew put his flute down and he and Caleb circled around the flock softly singing a lullaby. The men whispered to each other about the angels and the baby. Uncle Rueben left the fire and walked over to Caleb. He called quietly to Matthew, "Son, we are going to leave you boys in charge, while we go look for that baby. If we find the baby, you boys can go see him tomorrow when you deliver the sheep to market. Caleb, help your cousin keep a sharp eye on our sheep until you get sleepy." He tousled the little boy's tight curls and smiled at him.

The men strode away pointing to the star and looking ahead to the little town of Bethlehem. They went to find the babe.

It's A Deal!

By
Margaret Watland

Chapter One

Janesville, Wisconsin—October 1951

Tim Hunter sat at the table in his large square kitchen. A hot stew pot of three-day-old chili rested on a potholder in front of his soup bowl. A bread sack full of cornbread, butter, Tabasco Sauce and a cup of coffee was the whole of his supper. Usually he listened to the news but the radio beside him sat silent. The hands on the clock above him showed 8:30 PM.

Branches from the old maple tree brushed against the roof. The yard light showed his sign, Farmer's Mechanic, swinging to and fro in the wind. The drafty old farmhouse sucked in the cold. Snaps and creaks echoed throughout the house.

After supper the young man considered turning on the oil heater but shook his head and with a sigh trudged up the stairs to bed. The fifth step from the top snapped. Another board in front of his Uncle Henry's bedroom squeaked. The old man passed on almost a year ago. He needed to clean out that bedroom.

The next morning Tim finished his second cup of coffee when he heard a truck coming down the lane. Out the dining room window Tim saw his best friend, Bert Calhoun, had brought Chet Hartford to pick up his tractor. He clicked off the radio, grabbed his jacket and opened the door.

"Good morning gentlemen. Well Chet, your tractor is purring like a kitten. Now you'll have to quit lazing around and go to work," he teased.

"Thanks Tim. You surprised me when you called last night and said it was done. Can I write you a check?" asked Chet.

"Yes sir. All the paper work is down at the shop."

The three men walked down a path behind the house that led to new large building and a few minutes later Chet drove away on his newly repaired International Tractor.

"Tim, I want to make a deal with you," said Bert. "You know how everybody's been telling me I need to move on, to start dating? Well my sweet little imp of a daughter kinda' helped me out and now I have a date with Mavis Strong for Sunday night after the Gospel Sing."

Tim whooped with laughter, "Oh I love your little Pansy she keeps life interesting! Mavis would be a good catch for you. It's been three years since Holly died and—yes—you need to move on."

"How about you? You're twenty-five years old and don't even have a girl friend. Henry left you this farm and a big old house that needs to be filled with a wife and kids," lectured Bert.

"Women scare me! I get around them, my throat tightens up and I have to choke my words out. I don't even sound like me. But—well—I've been getting acquainted with Julie Montgomery at the library. She's not much over five feet tall and she's cute. I think we'd make a good fit. You big gangly six-foot guys don't have to worry how tall a girl is but I don't want some woman towering over me. Every time I walk beside you, I think we must look like Mutt and Jeff in the funny papers," said Tim

"Come on man, you're taller than Mutt! You come up to my shoulders and I happen to know you're stronger than an ox. Girls like guys with muscles," laughed Bert.

"Aren't you funny," said Tim with sarcasm. "I've been thinking about asking Julie out for a hamburger. I'm going to the library tomorrow. I'll talk to her about double dating. I need to memorize what I'm going to say. If I can get the first word out maybe the rest of the words will just kinda' fall out on their own. Ya' think?"

"Tim you are too much! Okay, you memorize what you're going to say and let's do a double date for this first time. Deal?"

"All right it's a deal," said Tim

"You know that Mavis and Julie are good friends? If we can't think of anything to say we can let the girls do the talking," chuckled Bert.

He opened the truck door and muttered, "I know it's time for me to start dating but it still feels like I'm cheatin' on Holly. Man, would you say a prayer for me?"

"I'll pray for you and you pray for me," said Tim. "We need God to work this out for us!"

Chapter Two

Tim walked into the library with a stack of books cradled under his arm fifteen minutes before closing time. Sylvia Crane, the head librarian, strode toward him, "Tim you're just the man to help us. Those boxes of books stacked by the front door are for the Senior Center and I'm already late for my grandson's birthday party. Could you take Julie and the boxes over there in your truck after closing? They have a couple of ladies ready to help Julie shelve all the books in the Center's library."

"Yes ma'am." Tim grabbed one of the boxes and said to Julie, "I'll start loading these while you finish up."

"Thanks. I only have a few more things to do here and we can be on our way." Minutes later Julie came out of the library and locked the big front door.

"You go ahead and find your crew while I bring in the boxes," said Tim as he parked his red pickup truck in front of the Senior Center. Two white haired ladies came out the front door. Emily Emerson waved and said, "Hi Julie, we're ready to work. Do you want us to carry in the books?"

"No Ma'am, these boxes are too heavy for you. I'll do the carrying and you can help Julie," said Tim as he grabbed a box and followed the chattering women into the building.

"What's Tim doing helping you?" asked Harriet Adams the town gossip. She leaned towards Julie's ear and whispered, "Are you . . ."

"No! Sylvia just asked if he would help," answered Julie.

Tim stood holding a box labeled *Mystery* and watched Julie's cheeks flush with embarrassment.

She turned to him a little flustered and said, "Tim why don't you put that box down over by the empty bookcase and Harriet can fill it with mysteries."

"Alphabetize them by the author's last name," she said to the woman with too many questions.

Tim chuckled when he got out of Julie's hearing. She looked so cute all bothered.

A few trips later he put the last box down beside Emily.

An older gentleman opened the dinning room door and called out, "Bingo starts in ten minutes."

The two women whipped around and looked at Julie. Harriet said, "We can finish this Julie, you don't have to stay any longer."

"All right ladies," laughed Julie. "Enjoy your Bingo."

"Tim," said Harriet, "I'm wondering if you would have time to do an errand for us? Some old-timers came by yesterday with a trunk full of stuff for the Tallman House."

Julie came up behind Harriet and said, "Oh goodie some more things! I'm on their historical committee. We advertised for artifacts from the 1800's to furnish all the rooms in the Tallman House. What a wonderful response! It's like opening a Christmas present each time we get another donation."

Harriet took Tim and Julie to a storage room.

"Ohhh, it's a immigrant trunk!" exclaimed Julie. She dropped to her knees and ran her fingers along the corner of the trunk. "Look Tim, the dovetailing is hand cut. This is a wonderful piece. I'm sure it's over a hundred years old."

"Let's see how heavy this is," said Tim lifting one end of the trunk. "I think this is too heavy for you and me Julie."

He stepped out the front door where George the janitor was raking fall leaves and said,

"George, could you give me a hand with this old trunk?"

"Oh good," he replied, "I was waiting until I could find some help. We'll put it in your truck and then I'll follow you over to the Tallman house in my car so I can help you take it inside."

When Tim slid into the truck Julie turned to him and said, "Most people my age aren't interested in old things but I love searching for heirlooms! I have Birdseye maple furniture in my bedroom that belonged to my great-great grandparents.

"I was raised with heirlooms. My parents have an heirloom apple orchard with a thousand trees and I've started growing heirloom apple trees at my place," he said with a big grin on his face.

Julie looked at him with a puzzled frown and said, "Are you teasing me or . . . ?"

"Well kind of, but not really," said Tim as he pulled up to the front of the old Tallman house. He winked at her and climbed down from his truck to help George with the trunk.

After George drove away Tim cleared his throat. He stood holding the handle of the passenger door and said to Julie, "I was wondering—well—it's getting close to supper time and I—well—would you like to go out for a hamburger?"

Julie flashed Tim a smile that deepened the dimple in her chin. "Yes, that would be nice. I like strawberry shakes too," she said boldly.

He handed Julie into the truck and walked around to his door blowing out a lung full of air. He did it! He asked her and she said yes.

Chapter 3

Bert Calhoun stood, legs apart, hands in hip pockets, staring at the headstone.

Holly Adelle Calhoun,
April 4, 1927 * July 15, 1948
Loving Wife and Mother

Looking toward heaven with sad eyes and a chin tight and determined, he started to talk to Holly.

"Honey, they tell me I have to move on. Pansy needs a mama and they say you would want me to find someone else to love. I know they're right but . . ."

"I've come to tell you about Mavis Strong . . ."

He sat down on the ground, and with arms wrapped around bent legs, pulled his body into a fetal position. The young widower bowed his head into the curl of his frame and prayed.

Finally he looked up and discovered long shadows of late afternoon.

Tim arrived at the Calhoun's for the last practice before the Gospel Sing. Little Pansy Calhoun ran to him with black braids flying and both arms up in the air. "Unca Timmy do you gots my Daddy?" she asked.

Tim sat his instruments down, grabbed the four year old and tossed her in the air. "No I don't gots your Daddy. Where'd he go?"

Outside two truck doors slammed. Bert and guitarist Milt Robinson came into the house. Mabel and Ed Calhoun looked towards their son with concerned faces.

"Sorry, it took longer than I thought," said Bert to his parents. "I'll tell you about it later. It looks like I have time to eat some supper while we wait for the rest of the group."

Tim let Pansy down and she ran towards her Daddy.

"Oh no you don't," said Mabel grabbing both black braids of the little girl following her Daddy into the kitchen. "It's time for your bath. When you are clean and dressed for bed you can come down and tell your Daddy and all the other music makers goodnight."

Ed stepped close to Tim's ear and quietly said, "Stick around afterwards."

Two more trucks drove in. The rest of the musicians had arrived. Bert came in with half a glass of milk and a mouthful of pork chop. He swallowed, washed it down with a slug of milk and put the empty glass on a nearby widow sill. Bert lifted the Bass from it's stand and a two hour practice session began.

Guitar, mandolin, bass, banjo and fiddle made glorious gospel music that seeped into every corner of the Calhoun house. At the end of the practice the musicians packed up their instruments and left for home. The house sighed into a peaceful silence. Ed and Mabel said their goodnights.

Tim looked at Bert and asked, "What's going on?"

"This dating thing," said Bert with a sigh. "I talked to Mom and Dad about it and they suggested I go out to the cemetery and talk to Holly.

"I sat down by her grave and told her all about Mavis and a bunch of other stuff. I got a lot of things off my chest. I think it helped! When I got through talking to Holly I spent the rest of the time praying and asking God for His perfect guidance. Mavis is a lovely young woman and I don't want to hurt her!"

"It sounds to me like you got good advice. I'm not ashamed to say I've talked to Uncle Henry a time or two," confessed Tim.

"Do you have anything to report to me?" asked Bert. "Did you ask her?"

"Yes sir. I'm surprised you didn't hear. We had hamburgers at Jane's Diner. It's easy to talk to her. She likes heirlooms. I told her I lived with heirlooms all my life and how I'm working on an heirloom apple orchard of my own. I had her going there for a while! We had a good laugh about that. She's . . . well, she's really . . . she's special!"

"Oh my! Man, she has put a spell on you! Now don't you get all sappy on me," said Bert giving Tim's shoulder a push. "What about the double date? You did ask her didn't you?"

"Yes sir, she liked the idea. Tomorrow afternoon Julie's going to show me all the things the Historical Committee is doing at the Tallman House and I'm going to her house for supper. I haven't met her Mother yet. I hope I don't spill food down my shirt."

Barbara's Stories

Barbara J. Bina

Barbara J. Bina currently lives in the Pacific Northwest. She likes writing almost as much as breathing. Married for over twenty-four years she and her husband enjoy traveling and camping in an RV.

In her professional life, she authored multiple IEEE technical papers and magazine articles dealing with Computer Software. After retiring, she had the time and proclivity for creative fictional writing. Barbara received Honorable Mention in Writer's Digest 78th Annual Writing Competition for two of her stories. She is currently writing a linked series of fanciful stories inspired by a truthful base, a collection of episodes from her childhood years in Minnesota and her life's love story.

Barbara owes a lot of her writing improvement to the senior critique group of which she is a founding member. Thanks are given to her husband, sister and friends for their constant encouragement.

The Blue Bunny

By
Barbara J. Bina

Seven-year-old Patsy appeared absorbed in the colorful process of decorating cut-out sugar cookies little belying the turmoil within her. After carefully taking a tray of hot cookies from the oven, Margaret glanced at her niece. Good, she thought. With everything that has happened to her recently, I am glad she is able to occupy herself with something fun for a while.

"How's it going?" Margaret asked hopefully.

"It's fine. This is nice," responded Patsy. "My mother never did this with me."

They'd spent the day together, just the two of them, making Easter sugar cookies. Margaret had a varied collection of cookie cutters. They chose a bunny, a cross, eggs, a chicken, flowers and a carrot for this joint venture. The aromas of cinnamon, nutmeg and vanilla filled the kitchen.

"This is the last batch to go into the oven," said Margaret. "Then I'm going to join you in the decorating. How many have you finished?" She looked at the table and saw several colorful cookies. Smiling, she noticed the little chickens were covered with yellow frosting and the carrots were properly orange with green tops. The sugared egg forms sported multiple colors with contrasting stripes and polka dots. Pure white icing with silver beads placed down the center decorated the cross. As Margaret watched, her niece picked up a bunny cookie and reached for the bowl of blue frosting. Dipping a spreader into the bowl, Patsy began to cover the bunny with blue.

This perplexed Margaret. She frowned and asked her, "Why are you coloring the bunny blue? I mean, it's pretty, but that's not its natural color."

"I know, Aunt Margaret. I'm making it blue, because this bunny is sad."

"Why is it sad?"

"Well, because its parents are dead and she doesn't know where they are."

Margaret sat quietly trying to decide what to say.

A month ago, Patsy's parents were killed in an automobile crash. Margaret was named executor guardian. Since then it had been a rushed thirty days getting her niece moved and settled into her house with a room of her own. She wanted to make her feel at home, but knew nothing could replace Patsy's regular house.

"Patsy, where do you think your parents are?" Margaret asked.

"I don't want to talk about it now."

"That's fine. But when you're ready, just let me know. Okay?"

Margaret took the last tray of cookies out of the oven and placed them on the cooling racks.

"All the cookies are baked. Now we can work on the decorations together," Margaret said. "I think I'll work on the flowers."

As Margaret watched, Patsy picked up another bunny and covered it with blue frosting also. How sad she thought. I feel so sorry for Patsy. What a tragedy she had to lose her parents at such a young age.

"Is that bunny sad also?" Margaret asked.

"Yes, just like the others. All the bunnies are sad today."

"Well that's all right. It's okay to be sad when you've lost someone."

"Aunt Margaret, I was thinking. You know how when we went to church last Sunday and the minister told us that Jesus rolled away the big rock. And he said that Jesus rose from the dead and went to heaven. Do you think my parents can rise from the dead and come back to me? Cause I know we buried them in the cemetery with a stone by their heads."

Margaret wondered how best to answer her niece.

"Well, honestly, no I don't think that'll happen. Jesus is a powerful special person. He does things that no one else can do. Your parents went to heaven and are with God right now. They miss you and will forever be watching over you, but they can't be here with you. I know they would want to be if they could, but that just can't happen. And Patsy, let me tell you that what you're feeling is normal. It's sad to lose your parents."

As Margaret watched, tears dripped off Patsy's cheeks. They dropped onto the little blue bunny dissolving the blue frosting that ran onto her fingers.

"Come over here dear. Let me give you a hug."

Patsy rushed into her aunt's arms and cried.

"You know Patsy, from now on life will be different for both of us. I love you and want you to know that I'm glad you're here with me. I'm not the same as your mother, but I hope you can love me too."

* * *

Years passed. With Margaret's love and teaching, Patsy grew into a beautiful well-rounded young woman. She married and had three children of her own. When the time came to bury her aunt, she cried as her second mother was put in the earth next to her own parents.

Every Easter she made cut-out sugar cookies. She was glad to share that special holiday event with her own children. Patsy always decorated her bunnies with blue frosting.

Three Points of View

By
Barbara J. Bina

Second Person Point of View:

To print a document, you should follow these steps:

1. Make sure there is paper in the printer
2. Go to the file marked "My Documents" on your computer
3. Right click on the file you wish to print
4. Left click on the instruction to print
5. Wait until the printing is complete
6. Retrieve your document from the printer

Third Person Point of View:

The heels of petite charming Nicky Francois made pointy noises as she strode through the computer room to the shared terminal station. She was going to update a recently written chapter in her life story after receiving helpful comments from her critique group. The eyes of three other people in the room intently watched Nicky as she approached the computer. Taking a seat at the small swivel secretarial roller chair, she swung around to face the terminal. Her smooth delicate fingers with their bright red nail polish caressed the keys. Observers swore the computer screen smiled at Nicky as she gently stroked the letters and made the modifications to her document. Normally, company rules did not allow employees to conduct personal business on the company computer, but

Nicky was head secretary to the boss and she could do whatever she liked. The three observers smiled and nodded at Nicky as they watched a professional at work.

When she was satisfied with her document changes, Nicky saved it to a file on the computer. By habit, she closed down the Word program and went to "My Documents" in order to print a copy that contained her recent changes. She identified the file, clicked on print and the printer came to life. Nicky watched as the printer flawlessly produced and perfectly stacked the eight pages of her document. If it could, the printer would have stapled them for her as well.

Nicky picked up the pages and happily clicked out of the room.

First Person Point of View:

From the doorway, I watched this procedure in detail. My new boss had given me a small collection of notes to type and print. I was a recent hire and unsure of the procedure to create a printed document in this new environment. OK, I thought, Francis Nicodemus you are up to this task.

I strolled over to the computer station. My earth shoes squeaked on the wood tile floor as I squished my way across the room. The small secretarial chair groaned as I fitted my ample behind onto the tiny seat. I set my large container of Pepsi on the desk. As I was about to put the hand written notes down beside it, the rollers on the chair moved out and the papers dropped onto the floor. Bending over to pick up the papers, the chair scooted even further away and I tumbled down to the floor. OK, I thought, Francis you can do this. There is no problem. I got up from the floor and began again. I smiled at the three people in the room, who were watching my progress. I was familiar with creating Word documents, but not in a group setting.

I swiveled the chair around to face the terminal, being careful to stay balanced in the awkward small thing, and opened up Word. As I typed the five pages into a document, I periodically sipped from my Pepsi container. Everything seemed to be going just fine. I clicked on print, in order to obtain a hard copy of my work and swiveled in the chair to watch the printer produce my document. As I turned, my hand hit the Pepsi container. It rocked, but stayed vertical.

The printer produced two pages and then a light went on "Out of Paper". OK, I thought, Francis you can do this. Just put more paper into the paper tray and continue. Beneath the printer were two cabinet doors where typically extra paper is stored. I opened one door, banged my knee and ripped my panty hose, but discovered this was where the paper was stored.

I loaded the paper tray and the printer started up immediately. However, I had not straightened the sheets. A piece of paper stuck in the unit causing a jam. The red light on top of the printer started to blink indicating something was wrong. When I tried to remove the sheet, it ripped in half. OK, I thought, Francis you can do this. Just hit the button to eject the paper. It worked.

I turned back to the terminal to re-initiate the printing and things looked better. The printer started again. My five-page document printed perfectly and was neatly stacked in the tray. However, the printer did not stop at five pages. It printed another five pages and then another five pages and again and again. As well, the printer seemed to me to be going faster and faster. I must have inadvertently requested multiple copies. The additional pages came out at lightning speed. All the copies flew out of the tray and soon covered the floor in front of the printer.

When the printing finally stopped, I got up to retrieve the excess paper. As I reached over, I knocked my container of Pepsi again. This time it fell to the floor, covering the white sheets of my document with brown goo. At this point, the other three people in the room were pointing and laughing. OK, I thought, Francis you can do this. I picked up the sticky mess and threw it all into a trash container.

I sat down again on the dreadful tiny swivel chair being careful this time that it did not scoot away on me. I looked at the terminal screen, which was blank. It seemed my Pepsi seeped through a crack in the floor tiles and shorted the electrical connection. The computer system was dead. Worse, I had not saved a copy of my work. Not one of the three observers, now visibly bent over in guffaw laughter came over to help me. I was not happy! OK, I thought, Francis you cannot do this.

I got up from the chair and headed back to my boss's office. OK, I thought, Francis you can hand-write your resignation letter.

Fountain Lake

By
Barbara J. Bina

When you camp in the beautiful outdoors, the lovely sights and sounds of nature abound. Examples are the deer that wander into the shadows near sunset, the crystal clearness of a close lake or stream, and the bird's constant chatter while tending to their young in the spring. Even observing the destructive wandering of your neighbor's RV as they are trying to park is a remarkable sight. My husband and I have been camping with a truck and travel trailer for over twenty years. In that time, there have been many amusing incidents of parking failure. Early on, we had our own misguided directions and frustrations. However, fortunately we did not hit anything.

Last summer we went on a joint camping venture with my sister and brother-in-law. It was their first time camping with their new travel trailer. We parked in the center of the campground at a Washington State Park and had a clear view of neighboring sites. On the second day, a rather large motorhome towing a car, entered the park and attempted to maneuver into its assigned site. It was a huge full hook-up space. The driver was to be the park host for the summer, the one who knows everything and helps other campers. The RV proudly proclaimed that he was a retired Naval Captain. He must like the water.

My husband set up two chairs and said to my sister and me, "Come over here beside me. Sit and watch."

"Why? What's going on?" we asked as we headed to the chairs.

"There's going to be a show," he said softly. "The Captain's going to park his motorhome. Just watch."

The Naval Captain successfully disconnected the towed car and proceeded to back his RV into his spot. Then he decided to swing his rig to the right. It meant the tail end of the RV went to the left and that was exactly where the water spigot pipe was. His vehicle took the pipe right out of the ground causing considerable damage to his RV. We watched in awe as the tremendous, now uncontained water pressure, turned this accident into a beautiful fountain.

"Oh my goodness!" exclaimed my sister. "How did you know that was going to happen?"

"Well," replied my husband. "I didn't know exactly what was going to occur. But with the speed he entered the park, I thought something would happen."

The flustered host scurried around his spot with his hands either on his hips or up in the air. He inspected the community bath building and talked to other nearby campers. It appeared that there was no place to turn off the water. While the fountain blasted its lovely spray into the air, creating small rainbows in the unusually sunny Washington day, the park host marched back to the check-in area. They had to call the park ranger. Evidently, only the ranger had the keys to the master water shut off. Meanwhile there was quite a nice lake developing in the park host's assigned site.

We sat, watched the commotion and humorously discussed the perils of parking in a campground. My husband said, "You have front row seats for the next show. Turn around and watch."

A giant new motorhome sped into the campground. He drove right past the check-in area and headed directly to his assigned spot. Not stopping to inspect the site, he quickly turned the RV around to park it. He proceeded to back in as fast as he had driven into the campground. His spot was next to the jetty rocks on the ocean side of the park. Soon we heard the scrape of a bumper, fender, and exhaust pipe against the jagged rocks. I suppose the site was just a bit shorter than what the driver had in mind. He pulled forward and then got out to look at the site and his expensive motorhome. More damage and more repair bills is what he got for his speedy parking job.

My sister exclaimed, "This is quite a show!"

"I guess." I told her, "It shows what can happen when you're driving too fast. Parking an RV is a risky business. It's a good lesson for you."

Eventually the park ranger arrived and shut off the water. It meant no one on that end of the campground had water or showers that evening. Several campers were not happy. We, however, enjoyed the water show and the ever-expanding fountain lake.

Motorists are usually tired near the end of the day, and it is a time to be extra careful. There are a lot of RV's that have back-up cameras. This enables a clear visual image of what the rig is approaching while backing up. However, I think some drivers do not use them. I have seen motorhomes, even with spotters walking alongside their rigs, back right into a carefully placed and visible obstacle.

Just last month, on our way to Oregon, we were looking for a spot to stay for the evening. We pulled into a possible campground, but it had tighter spots than we liked. Inside the park, trying to maneuver around the loop to get to his site was a very large motorhome. As we watched, he made a left turn and ran the entire side of his RV along a cement barrier pole. At that point, his wife and another traveling companion got out to help give him directions. The driver thought it necessary to back up and swing the RV around. Misjudging the errant back end of the RV, he backed right into a cement and wooden fence causing considerable damage on the other side of his RV. We wondered if that would count as one or two accidents when he talked to his insurance agent. The driver was so flustered at this point that he mistakenly hit a button, which sent his enormous RV slide-out out. Fortunately, it stopped just short of hitting yet another post. We decided this park was not for us, and took our leave. While exiting, after going around a different rather tight loop ourselves, we saw the same large RV still trying to get out of the park. The driver now had considerable more help from numerous additional spotters. Luckily, we found a roomy campground just a few more miles down the road.

The next day we reached our destination campground in Oregon. I had made reservations at this particular facility, because they offered a WiFi service. I specifically had requested and pre-paid for site #28 after being told it had reliable reception. When we arrived, another truck and travel trailer was at the check-in area. While we waited, I told my husband to look at their travel trailer. The owner must have had difficulty parking in the past. Above the trailer wheel-well was a recently replaced shiny new three-foot protection guard. However, the driver had hit it since the repair because it was crumpled.

"We'd better give them lots of room," my husband acknowledged. "Looks like they've had trouble turning their RV."

After getting their site number, the people got into their truck and proceeded to their spot. We entered the office to sign in for our space.

"You're already here," the campground owner said to me with a confused smile on her face. "You registered three days ago. And, because of that, I just gave space #28 to the family which just checked in."

"No," I replied. "I'm here now for the first time, and I definitely need site #28. I've already paid for it, and I need the WiFi connection."

"Well, that's odd that there would be two people with the same name at my campground," she muttered while riffling through her registration papers.

She hustled out to site #28 and told the new occupants they must take a different space. This required that they drive around the entire outside loop of the campground to get back to the registration area. The driver did this while leaving his trailer steps down and the door to the travel trailer open. This can be dangerous to the rig.

When the driver reached the check-in area again, he stopped, got out and went in to re-register. I told my husband to make sure they had enough room to proceed around our truck and travel trailer. My husband walked over, put up the other man's trailer stairs and closed the trailer door, thereby reducing some of the extra width. After obtaining a different site, the driver took off and shortly we all heard a crash. He had swung too tight. Again, that long errant trailer rear end had veered out causing unexpected damage. He decimated a whiskey barrel full of flowers as well as a sign, which read "SWING WIDE". It also took out the plastic drainpipe for the sewer connection on his trailer, which was not going to be usable until repaired. He limped over to his new site.

The following day my husband went over to talk to the man about his trailer's damage wanting to see if he needed any assistance in the repair. He received such an unexpected response. I am still shocked at it.

The other man said, "No, thank-you, I have had enough of you already. Your wife, who had to insist on site #28, caused all this damage to my travel trailer."

My husband replied, "Well, you have a nice day."

I wanted to go over and have a few words with the man myself, but my husband stopped me. In retrospect, I believe that was probably the better side of prudence.

Therefore, when you sit and ponder the beautiful birds and the views one can have during camping; consider there are other remarkable adventures just lurking around the next turn.

Madeline

By
Barbara J. Bina

Throughout high school, in the small town of Providence, Iowa, Madeline dreamed about going to New York City and becoming a successful actress. Whenever she could afford to buy a copy of "Star Highlights" magazine, she read it from cover to cover and fell asleep with the stars from the lights on Broadway in her eyes. Her drama teacher told her she had great potential, but that it would take a lot of hard work, and even more luck to become famous in the theater, particularly in New York City. Nevertheless, Madeline would not be deterred.

During her senior year, she dated a fellow student named Jimmy. He listened to her rattle on about being a big star, but figured it was just a phase. They were getting very serious and surely, this nonsense about becoming an actress would fade, he thought. Jimmy felt Madeline and he were made for each other. He would provide for all her happiness.

"Madeline," Jimmy insisted, "you belong here in Providence. This is your home."

However, at their high school graduation party, she told her close friend Naomi that she was going to the Big Apple within a month and launch her career. That is exactly what she did. Amidst the tears of her mother, the warnings of her father and the disbelief of Jimmy, she set off on a Greyhound bus for New York City.

Upon her arrival, the huge buildings, lack of greenery, enormous number of people, fast pace, number of taxicabs and the noise was overwhelming. Her mother told her to go to the YWCA for lodging, as it was reasonably priced and hopefully safe. After standing for a short time on the busy street and looking around in awe at the change in her surroundings, Madeline hailed a cab and rode to the local Y. There she checked in and paid for her first month of accommodations. That night she fell asleep with a smile on her face, and real NYC lights in her eyes. The next morning she was up early and excited to begin her first day. She picked up a map of the subway system and bought a copy of "Casting Digest," a specialized newspaper which had current lists of available auditions and casting calls. Jotting down a few that looked interesting, Madeline headed out to find the theaters. These were not main-line Broadway theaters, but off-Broadway and off-off-Broadway. She thought to herself, well, you have to start somewhere.

The casting directors at the first two theaters said the roles that would be appropriate for her were filled. Well, that's fine, thought Madeline. It's understandable. Perhaps the paper didn't have the updated information. She received the same answer at three more theaters. I still have one more theater to find this afternoon, she thought, and maybe that'll work. However, she received the same result. Next week, she figured, surely next week something will be more promising. However, it was not to be. Every week she bought the theater rag, perused the openings, went to the auditions, and got nowhere except turned down. Some of the directors told her about a fancy gentleman's club that was hiring young ladies, but Madeline just shook her head. That was not something she wanted to do. The month had almost passed, and her resolve was crumbling.

She had carefully planned her money to last for the first month. She figured with all the promise and talent she possessed, that she would get an immediate part in a play, if even small, and earn enough to make ends meet after that. Besides being disillusioned, she was also running desperately low on funds. Daily she counted her money to see how much she could spend on food and transportation. I don't want to admit to my parents that I am a failure, she thought. Nor do I want to have to admit to Jimmy that he was right. I don't want to give up my dream. I've wanted to be an actress all my life. Perhaps something will turn up, she hoped. Maybe my lucky break will come soon.

Today was four weeks since Madeline had come to New York City. It was noon and the end of another unsuccessful morning of talking to casting directors. Being downtown, and close to Washington Square, she stopped to buy a hot dog and soda from a street vendor. She counted out her coins, paid for her lunch and walked into the park to find a place to sit.

As Madeline entered, she noticed a black teenage boy and an elderly black woman, who looked like she could have been his grandmother, walking towards each other. They stopped face to face. The boy was dressed in baggy low-hanging black jeans, with the cuffs scraping the pavement. He had a black over-sized tee shirt with some sort of red and yellow dragon design on the front. A long chain that looped around his waist dangled almost to his knees. Silver heavy rings adorned his fingers. The elderly woman was large and dressed in a purple floral loose fitting dress. She clutched a large stained navy blue fabric purse and wore old red laced mid-heeled shoes, which turned to the outside from excess wear. She stood with her hand on her hip and one foot out in front of the other. The teenage boy had both hands in his pockets. He stood slightly slouched with his head cocked at an angle and one shoulder slightly raised.

"Hi," the woman said to the young boy.

"Hi," he replied.

"Where were you?" the older woman asked angrily.

"Nowhere."

"What do you mean nowhere? I've been in this park for forty-five minutes. Did you forget you were supposed to meet me here?" she asked.

"Nah, I was just busy."

"What do you mean busy? What's the matter with you anyway? Why don't you have any respect for your grandmother? Why do I always have so much trouble with you? You're a good-for-nothing," she said while throwing her hands into the air.

"Oh, shut up old woman," spat the boy. "You ain't got any business telling me what to do."

Madeline politely averted her eyes from this agitated conversation, and continued to walk by. She thought, no one in Providence would act like that. Both of them showed such disrespect to the other.

Ambling further into the park Madeline found two park benches setting side by side. A young woman, about her age, sitting on one bench was continually scanning the walkways. Madeline chose to sit by herself on the second bench. A young man approached the lone woman.

"Hi," he said to her, with a wide smile on his face.

"Hi," she replied coquettishly.

"Where were you?"

"Nowhere," she replied, "I've been here for about an hour, just waiting for you."

"I thought we were going to meet at your apartment."

"Well, I was tired of studying and felt like getting some air. I knew you would be walking through the park. So, I thought that I might catch you here."

"I'm glad you did," he replied.

The man bent over, gave the woman a kiss on the cheek, and sat down beside her. "I wanted to talk about us moving in together. Do you think you're ready for that step in our relationship?" he asked her.

A broad smile came over her face as she nodded her head. Their conversation grew quieter as they took turns whispering into each other's ears and giggling in return.

As Madeline slowly munched her hot dog, she thought about the two different conversations she had just heard. They had the same start, but one was filled with anger, and one was filled with happiness. Whatever am I doing here in New York? I truly miss Jimmy and want to go back to Providence, where people are nice to each other and happy in love. Madeline got up and threw the remainder of her hot dog into the trash. She returned to the YWCA and phoned her parents to ask if they would arrange for a return bus ticket back to Providence. Then she phoned Jimmy to tell him she was coming home. He was happy, and now so was Madeline. As she packed her bag, she tossed out the old copies of "Casting Digest", and with them tossed out her aspirations of being a famous actress. She went outside, got a cab to the bus station and never looked back.

Fireworks of a Different Nature

By
Barbara J. Bina

Amidst the oppressive Philadelphia summer heat, visiting crowds anxiously anticipated the Independence Day evening fireworks extravaganza. Unrecognized was a fire igniting in a young girl's heart.

In the Italian section of South Philadelphia, sixteen-year-old Mariella lay on her pink and white chenille covered twin bed reading a back issue of *Teen Star Magazine*. She avidly followed the movie stars' romantic adventures. Daydreaming, she wondered if true love would ever find her. Mariella was shy, overweight and bursting to become an adult. She had always been plump and was bitterly teased when she was in grade school. The cruel words hurt then as much as they did now.

Her mother sympathized, "Mariella, don't worry about it. You're just healthy. It's only baby fat."

Now being a teenager and getting seriously interested in boys, her figure had become even more important to her. She tried not eating, without any success in losing weight. She tried fad diets, but they did not work. How could they when her mother told her, "Finish everything on your plate, dear. Think of all the young children that don't have enough to eat."

Mariella knew a carnival had been running in downtown Fairmont Park for a week. Today was July 4 and tonight the fireworks were going to be lit off in the park. A few days ago, she had asked her mother, "Do you think it would be all right if I were to go to the carnival with my friend Sophia? And then, could we maybe stay downtown for the evening show?"

It was 1976, the year of the nation's Bicentennial. All of America had celebrated its birth with commemorative festivities over the past year. The US Treasury minted special quarters, half dollars and silver dollars. Locally citizens painted their fire hydrants and mailboxes red, white and blue. The American Freedom Train traveled through the contiguous forty-eight United States. Tall ships sailed into several East Coast ports. Even Queen Elizabeth and her husband Prince Philip visited America. What better place to be than in Philadelphia where some two hundred years ago the Declaration of Independence was adopted. Festivities had been going on for months. Philadelphia hosted multitudes of visitors who came to see Independence Hall. A celestial extravaganza of fireworks was to culminate the festivities.

Philadelphia was hot. It had been in the high eighties and nineties all week. At the carnival, standing next to the shooting gallery, the carny man's black eyes slowly surveyed the crowd. A deep tan almost disguised the two days growth of facial hair. Wavy black hair that covered his head reached just below his ears. It swept to the back on the sides. The red and blue short-sleeved cotton shirt was unbuttoned showing a gray-tinged white undershirt. Black curly hairs bristled from the curved top of the undershirt. I'll be glad to get out of this town tomorrow, he thought. It'll be good to be back on the road again. A potential customer, a "mark", approached the shooting gallery.

"Try your luck, mister?" yelled the carny man. "Keep the shots in the bull's eye and win a radio for the missus? Three tries for only a dollar. I'll throw in an extra for free, just for you. Four for the price of three. How about it?" The man shook his head and walked on. "Tight wad," the carny man mumbled to himself.

Mariella's parents had talked it over and decided that it would be all right for her to go to the festival. She was now sixteen and should be trusted with a little more independence. She knew the bus routes. She would be able to get home okay. A girl ought to have some freedom and her friend is a good girl. Sophia is more than a year older and more experienced. She will watch out for her. The two of them should be all right.

For hours, the two friends talked about what to wear. Mariella decided on a simple light blue cotton dress, tied at the waist with a red band. Sophia chose a red skirt with a tight dark blue top. They both wore white tennis shoes. They were excited to be going to the festival. It was the first time she would be out and on her own that late at night. When her father offered to drive them to the park, she refused saying, "I'd rather take the bus, Dad. We will be okay." She wanted as much time out on her own that she could get.

"Be safe, Mariella," her mother fussed. "Here, take this ten dollar bill and put it inside your shoe. Use it to get a taxi back home if you need to. And, here's are some extra coins in case you need to call us. Put them in your pocket. Do you think you'll need a sweater? It might get chilly tonight. And here, I fixed a small sandwich for you and Sophia to take with you in case you get hungry."

"Gee, thanks Ma," she smiled and replied. "I'll be fine. I gotta go now. I've got to get to Sophia's house. I told her I'd be there by two."

After she kissed her parents goodbye and turned the corner, she threw the brown paper bag with the sandwiches into the trash. She practically flew to her friend's house. She was elated to be on her way.

The two friends spent the afternoon on amusement rides like the Ferris Wheel, Tilt-a-Whirl and the Swinger. In between rides, they wandered around the grounds or sat on benches, talking and watching people.

"I'm hungry," Sophia finally said. "Let's get a hotdog and soda."

"Great," Mariella responded. "I'm hungry too."

They walked up to the stand and bought their meal.

"Let's sit over there on the park bench. Wasn't that hotdog guy cute?" Sophia giggled and asked.

"I'll say. This is so much fun."

The aromas of the dry wood shavings, cotton candy, popcorn and cooking grills filled their noses. The carnival calliope music, the screams from the rides and the noise from barkers calling out to potential customers was thrilling. It was exciting to be out together just by themselves.

"Hey, let's go and see if we can win a stuffed animal," Mariella said.

"That sounds like fun. Let's go! I still have some money left. It's on the other side of the rides, I think."

The carny man stood leaning against the shooting gallery's exterior wall. His right foot lay casually crossed in front of his left. In his left hand, he held a cigarette between the index finger and thumb with the lit end in towards his palm. His ring finger snapped against the cigarette knocking the ashes to the trampled grassy ground. Smoke curled lazily up towards his face. When he took a drag on the cigarette, he held the smoke inside before exhaling through his nose. Tight worn black denim slacks hung low on his hips. The thumb on his right hand was crooked onto one of the belt loops. His fingers constantly rubbed slowly against his hipbone.

The carny man saw Mariella before Mariella saw him. He watched her walk with her friend near to his stand. When Sophia left to go get a chocolate nut covered ice cream, he made his move.

"Hey," he said. "How ya' doing?"

Mariella glanced around trying to see who was talking.

"Are ya' liking the events? It's quite something, ain't it?" He said.

She asked wide-eyed, "Are you talking to me?"

"Sure. Who else?"

His words caused an excited twitter inside her. Here was a stranger, a good-looking man talking to her! This was something she had not experienced before. He was treating her like an adult, like a woman who talked to a guy every day.

"It's great. I mean I love being here. It's quite a festival, isn't it?" Mariella replied.

"Ya' wanna try to shoot something here in this gallery?"

"Oh, I don't know."

"I can help you aim, just come on over. I'm Jim. What's your name?"

"Well, I'm waiting for my friend. I don't know." Where was Sophia, she thought.

"It's okay. She can find us. We'll be right here. We're not going anywhere. Do you live around here?"

"Close. I live in South Philadelphia," she said approaching him.

She was cautious but aroused. This was the first time an unknown guy had paid any particular attention to her. It made her feel special and grown-up. She smiled inwardly. It excited her. It made her feel like a woman.

"Well, maybe," she said. "But I don't have much money."

"It's okay," the carny man said as he dropped his cigarette and smashed it into the ground. "We don't charge for lessons for beginners. Come on over here closer. Let me show you how to hold the gun." He picked up a rifle and handed it to her. Then he put his arm around her. He smelled of smoke, leather, sweat and a musky aftershave.

"First you hold it like this," he said snuggling in close to her.

When Sophia returned from getting her ice cream, she watched her friend talking to the carny man and quickly stepped in.

"Mariella," she said. "What's going on?"

"Hi Sophia. Jim's going to show me how to shoot the guns."

The carny man thought, oh boy, a double header. How lucky can I get?

He said, "Sophia, maybe you'd like to shoot also. There's no charge for pretty girls such as yourselves. Come on Mariella."

"No, I think my friend and I'll be moving along. Come on Mariella."

Bewildered, Mariella put down the rifle and stared at her friend.

"Hey I didn't mean to offend you. Don't go away mad. Come on. Let me make it up to you," the carny man pleaded.

"We'd better just leave. Come on."

Further, as the two of them walked through the rest of the carnival, Mariella asked her friend, "Why did you want us to leave? I think he really liked me."

Sophia did not know what to say in response. "I just didn't like him. I thought it best if we moved on."

She did not ask again about her friend's decision to leave. Her own emotions were confusing her. As they walked along, Sophia thought Mariella was enjoying the carnival. They went on a few more of the rides and it seemed they were having fun. In reality however, Mariella was brooding about the flirtation with the carny man.

It was getting late and the two friends wandered over close to where the igniting of the fireworks was to take place. The ignitions officer was busy screaming orders to the shooters. Setting up the firework rounds was important. The team was excited that their performance was soon to begin. The sun set at 8:00 p.m. and darkness settled in. It was not long before the operators started setting off the canisters.

The pungent smell of the gunpowder from the fireworks was overwhelming. It hung low in the sky like a fog and barely danced through the park with the almost nonexistent breeze. Temporarily Mariella's thoughts drifted to the Revolutionary War held two hundred years ago. Was this what it was like on the battlefield, when our soldiers were fighting the British? Did the gunpowder firing from their rifles create smoke this thick back then also? Did they hear as much thunder from the shooting as I am hearing tonight?

Black speckles of gunpowder residue floated and spotted her blue cotton dress. When the fireworks lit up the night, she was awestruck. They were directly beneath the gigantic multicolored explosions. Sometimes she could feel the hot ash as it landed on her bare arms after falling from the sky. It brought her back to the present.

Mariella watched the shooters light the fuses and run back thirty feet. She saw the highlighted anticipation in their faces, coupled with the knowledgeable fear of what could happen if the lighting went wrong. She sensed the firing and the exotic lofty results of their actions made evident in the sky aroused them. They treated the firing carefully like handling a pet dragon once docile but now too big for its cage. The sound of the explosions was near deafening. She had never been this close to such an impassioned event before. Her body shuddered each time the fireworks were lit, propelled into the sky and exploded.

The fireworks were indeed spectacular that evening. They lighted and illuminated the entire city of Philadelphia. Mariella's parents watched the spectacle from the front porch of their brick row house thinking about their young daughter somewhere out there on her own.

Sophia and Mariella were overwhelmed with the fireworks. The entire day had been exciting for them both. They were happy to be experiencing the exploding tribute to America in such an intimate setting. The display was a fitting conclusion to the Bicentennial festivities. However, the fireworks were just a small candle compared to the fire ignited in Mariella's heart earlier in the afternoon.

Jason Angelina Tobias

By
Barbara J. Bina

Half silently singing and kicking the fallen leaves out of his way, Jason strutted along the crowded New York City street. People passed, but could hardly hear his words:

> *It's been a hard day's night*
> *And I've been working like a dog.*
> *It's been a hard day's night*
> *I should be sleeping like a log.*
> *But when I get home to you,*
> *I find the things that you do*
> *Will make me feel alright.*[1]

It was Saturday. The normally busy avenue was closed to automobile traffic. The Upper East Side community hosted an autumn Labor Day festival. People walked down the middle of the street and shopped at the varied booths. Vendors sold leather purses and wallets, jewelry, blown glass, antique furniture, fabric goods, paintings, and the like. Food stands sold gyros, hotdogs, caramel apples, cider, ice cream and other fun foods. Their inviting smells filled the air. Small bands played

---

[1] Lennon, John. "A Hard Day's Night." *A Hard Day's Night.* United Artists, 1964.

various types of music much to the delight of the customers. It was a festive event.

Jason repeated the Beatles' song lyrics as he shuffled along. " . . . *Will make me feel alright.* Yes, that's right Chiquita. You could make me feel alright," he mumbled to himself as he saw an attractive young lady standing alone near by the corner. His eyes slowly ran from the top of her dark brown hair down to her candy apple red high heeled sling-backed shoes. This might be a good day for me yet, he thought to himself as he approached the young woman.

Jason, an unmarried fifty-three year old man, lived at home with his mother. He was short about five feet six. His full grey mustache, trimmed to just above his upper lip, was lighter in color than his sparse grey-black streaked hair. He wore a white tee shirt with the words *Just ask me . . . I'm Great!!* printed on the front. Over the tee shirt was a green and gold nylon windbreaker that had oil stains on the sleeves. He wore dark blue, new, straight-legged jeans that ballooned out over his legs and swished when he walked. Jason enjoyed the sound. He thought it announced his presence, like a drumroll. He liked to stand out. On his feet were white and red dirty sneakers.

Jason worked part time for a shoe repair shop. Today his boss told him to leave because business was slow. During his walk through the festival, he had stepped on a sticky caramel apple wrapper that someone had dropped on the ground. It stuck to his shoe and followed him like an errant piece of toilet paper all the while making crackling noises as he walked. However, Jason was unaware that it was there because the swishing noise of his jeans was louder than the crinkling of the paper. Fortunately, somewhere, before he reached the street corner the piece of paper came loose from his shoe.

Jason approached the young lady and leaned carelessly, but confidently against the street sign. He smiled at her, showing a leftover piece of green lettuce stuck between his yellow teeth.

"Hey there," Jason said. "I was wondering if you'd like . . ."

In the middle of the sentence, the woman in the high-heeled red shoes slightly turned her head, glanced down at Jason with a grimace and promptly walked off. She sauntered down the street in the direction from which Jason had come. He shrugged and watched her walk away.

Angelina was used to being directly approached by men, although she did not like it. Having a face like an angel, as her mother said, being tall, twenty-five, and having a good figure, she knew she was desirable. Her long dark brown hair had a bit of a reddish glint that glistened in the autumn sunshine. Today with the addition of a tight red skirt, a loose fitting low-cut red and white cotton blouse, and the new red high-heeled shoes she knew she was particularly attractive.

As Angelina walked away from the annoying short man at the corner, she unknowingly stepped on the sticky caramel apple wrapper that had come loose from his shoe. She did not know it was there because her chin was haughtily stuck in the air as she walked with her eyes averted to some imaginary sight above. The paper crinkled as she walked, but Angelina could not hear it. A nearby band was loudly playing old Beatles' tunes and the music drowned out the noise made by the paper.

Approaching the band, she added an extra sway to her stride. The music was peppy and enjoyable. She had hoped to meet a nice good-looking young man at the fair today. There were many people on the street. This festival, held once a year attracted a lot of attention. The Upper East Side of New York City was the place to meet doctors, lawyers and stockbrokers her friends told her. Angelina had recently broken up with her boyfriend and she was ready for a new relationship.

When she got close to the band, the music took over. Angelina put her hands in the air and turned circles to the beat. As the song ended, on her last turn, the sticky paper came loose from her shoe. When the music stopped, she stood still, her breast slightly heaving as she was getting her breath.

A paunchy bulldog that had gotten loose from his owner ran directly towards her. It startled Angelina and she gave a little yelp. As she backed quickly away, her heel caught on a hole in a grate and broke off. Angelina stumbled, but fortunately did not fall to the ground. The dog started licking at the caramel apple wrapper, trying to extract the sugary sweetness.

"Tobias, Tobias you come back here," cried a tall attractive young man who was obviously running after the dog. "I'm sorry, Miss. Are you all right? My dog got away from me."

"I'm fine, but my new shoe is broken," Angelina moaned.

"Let me get it fixed for you," he said. "It's entirely my fault. Well, my fault and Tobias's fault, I guess. I know there's a repair shop just down the block. I live close. Do you think you could manage to walk there, if I help you?"

"I think so, if it's not too far," Angelina said. "I need to get it fixed."

"I couldn't help but notice you're enjoying the music," he said as they started hobbling towards the repair shop.

"Yes, it's great. I love music of all kinds," she said with a smile. So you live in the neighborhood, Angelina thought. I wonder where you work.

Tobias ate the sticky caramel wrapper, paper and all, and traipsed after them.

A Late Night Read

By
Barbara J. Bina

It was late Halloween evening. The doorbell had finally stopped announcing little white ghosts, bloody monsters and skeletons carrying their plastic orange pumpkins. I decided to shut off the porch light, fix a quick meal and turn in for the night. Last evening I started reading an intriguing book and was anxious to continue. I fluffed the pillows, got into bed, opened my book and began to read. I hung on every word until the outside world disappeared.

Next thing I knew, I awoke with the book by my side and my blankets in disarray. The window was open. I could see it was still dark outside. Apparently, I had fallen asleep with the night light on. I remember going to bed about midnight with a snack and my book. It was an unusually warm October evening. I must have kicked the thin covers from my feet.

I felt something brush against me. My surprise turned to horror when I looked down and saw a bloody burned decaying hand with only a thumb and two remaining fingers slowly caressing my ankle. Frozen by unspeakable fear my muscles could hardly respond as I desperately tried to slide my foot away from that ugly repulsive thing. I was alone in bed, or so I had thought, and the soft embrace from this terror in the night must have awoken me. In the midst of the stroking, it would pause and the tip of its index finger would slowly move in an insane erotic clockwise motion.

As I watched this putrid piece of flesh tenderly fondle my skin I was so petrified that I could not cry out. I was afraid if I jerked my leg too quickly away or if I were to scream, the hand would quickly curl its fingers around my leg and lock itself into a permanent embrace.

I lay there in sickened silence, watched, and felt the repulsive near bony hand slowly stroke my ankle. The smell in the room was overwhelming, sort of sweet and pungent at the same time like the coppery fragrance of fresh meat when first placed on a preheated barbecue grill. It was so strong I could taste it in the very back of my throat. I wondered, am I truly awake? Or is it possible that I am in the horrific center of a nightmare? I glanced at the crescent moon that shone through the thin window sheers. What am I to do? Oh, what am I to do?

I tightly closed my eyes and prayed that the monster with which I was now sharing my bed would disappear. I heard a coyote howl in the distance and a crash as something large flew against the window. To my surprise, the fondling stopped and the aroma vanished. I opened my eyes with timid trepidation and looked down at my foot. The hand too had disappeared. The window sheers were gently swaying. My silent prayers were answered. In thanks, I vowed to stop taking sardines to bed and to stop reading Stephen King books so late at night, particularly on Halloween.

The First Thanksgiving

By
Barbara J. Bina

I read somewhere that a family placed an empty chair at their Thanksgiving table to reserve a place for a loved one that was no longer there. That is not what we did.

My sister used to host our Thanksgiving gathering. All the family would bring assigned foods to share. Our feast was typical of modern day Thanksgiving meals. Turkey, stuffing, cranberry sauce, mashed potatoes, gravy, rolls, relish tray and salads were on the menu every year. My mother always brought a fruit salad made with pineapple jello, fruit cocktail, whipped cream, canned pineapple, bananas and marshmallows. Depending upon a relative's interest, they might bring sweet potatoes, cottage cheese, green bean casserole or baked corn pudding.

After we finished washing the dishes, under my mother's direction, we would use the leftover mashed potatoes to make Lefse, a traditional Norwegian flatbread. It reminded her of her own childhood Thanksgiving. She wanted to pass that tradition onto us. We completed the day by making annual Christmas ornaments, bridging our family into the next big holiday.

Our family celebration always included my pies. I made at least five pies: two pumpkin, one mincemeat (Dad's favorite) and two more of my choosing. It might be banana cream, blueberry, apple, cherry, huckleberry, or peach. One year I dyed the pastry dough green and used it for a raspberry pie, to symbolize the red and green of Christmas.

Probably baked corn was the only same food served for The First Thanksgiving at Plymouth Rock in 1621. From my research, they did not serve turkey. Cranberry sauce and mashed potatoes were not even known at that time. More than likely the fare included venison brought by the Wampanoag Indians. The Pilgrims probably cooked roast duck, seafood, cabbage, onions, corn and squash. These were good healthy hearty fare from the autumn's bounty.

As Mother became increasingly ill and could no longer easily travel to my sister's house, the Thanksgiving family dinner transferred to my home because Mom lived closer to me. I found it was no easy chore to prepare the house and entertain up to fifteen people. My admiration grew for my sister who had hosted so many holidays in the past years.

The family always had an enjoyable time. We ate, played games, ate, made Christmas decorations, ate, divided the left overs, ate, played cards (poker was my mom's favorite) and ate some more. One year I decided to host a mixed up Thanksgiving. We had cranberry pie, pumpkin soup, hot potato salad and cooked the turkey upside down in the oven.

My mom died just a few days short of her eightieth birthday. I somewhat believe she gave up life just so she did not have break into another decade. The family anticipated her death since she had been ill for many years. Regardless, it was still a sad shock. This occurred only two months before the Thanksgiving holiday. How different it would be now. We all talked about the new family situation.

One family member asked, "What should we do? Should we return to having Thanksgiving at my sister's house?"

We wondered if a different locale would diffuse the sad reality of the missing matriarch. This would be the First Thanksgiving without her being there.

By joint decision and after consulting with my father, of course, we decided it would be best to continue to meet at my house. It would be easier for Dad to get there and my home had now become the traditional holiday meeting place.

My dad said, "Life does go on, even after the death of someone close." Thus, it was decided.

The holiday approached with quiet reserve. My relatives arrived mostly on time bringing their assigned foods. Dad made and brought Mother's fruit salad. I forget how many family members were present.

Many last minute preparations kept my sisters and me busy during the morning. The grandchildren played games. The men watched television. Finally, with the table set, water glasses filled, turkey carved, potatoes mashed, salads placed and serving dishes arranged, it came time to take our seats at the dining room table. We sat down and all were quiet. No one spoke. It was deeply different not having Mother there. Dad gave the table prayer. This year we prayed for those who could not be present, and also those who would not be present. A few tears were shed. I thought to myself, there would come a day when Dad will not be at this table either.

We did not set an empty chair at the table for my mother. We did not have to do that. We knew she was with us. She would not have missed our family Thanksgiving get together for anything. As we were eating, I remembered something my aunt had once told me and shared it with my family at the table.

I related, "When people die, they are not really gone. You keep them alive in your heart by remembering them. All we love becomes a part of us."

We missed Mom's presence, but we managed to get through The First Thanksgiving. We even had an enjoyable time.

Stranger in the Park

By
Barbara J. Bina

Roberta plopped down onto a city park bench and started to cry. She pulled her sweater tightly around her front. This morning the cold wind whipped the trees and fluttered their yellow leaves to the ground. It was typical for a September day in Rittenhouse Square, Philadelphia, but it was not the cold that bothered her. The end of the month was soon here and she did not have money for next month's rent. She barely had enough to feed her five-year-old daughter, Susie, who was innocently playing on the swings across the park, as she watched. Roberta fingered the few remaining dollar bills that lay at the bottom of her thin sweater pocket. Sometimes I just feel like giving up, she thought. How am I going to get by? What are we going to do if we lose our apartment? Winter is soon here. Where can I get a warm coat for my child? The fear of failure lay heavy on her mind. I do not know how I am going to resolve this dilemma, Roberta thought.

She sat hunched over with her head in her hands and tears in her eyes. Roberta reminisced about how things had so quickly changed. Last year at this time, I was employed and had somewhere to be every day. I liked my job at the jewelry and coin shop. Life was going well for me. I was able to afford day care for Susie. We were happy. My boss said I could expect a promotion soon. Yet earlier this year everything changed. Instead of getting a promotion, I received a pink slip. Still I think I made the right decision not to give in to his demands. However, here I am now with difficult decisions to make.

As Roberta watched, a dirty white whiskered homeless man walked from the right side of the park and approached her daughter. His long tattered hounds-tooth coat flopped in the wind as he paused and stood beside Susie. He had no hat, nor scarf. The wind whipped his uneven uncut white hair around and hid his face. The angle of his position was such that he cut off the sight line to her little girl.

"Susie, Susie," Roberta cried out with alarm as she hastily rose from the park bench and started walking in her daughter's direction. "Susie, come here," she yelled out with a note of fear in her voice. The old man turned towards Roberta. She could see that he had his hands around one of her daughter's hands. The man gave Roberta a toothy grin showing surprisingly white teeth and patted Susie's hand. Roberta sped up and watched in horror as he bent down towards her daughter as if whispering something to her. Then he hurriedly walked off.

Roberta reached her daughter. "Susie, did he hurt you?" she asked.

"No, Mother. I'm all right."

"Did he say something to you? What did he say?"

"He told me everything is going to be all right. Then he put this pretty coin into my hand." Susie handed it to her mother. "I think that old man was nice, Mother," she said.

Looking at the yellow shiny coin protected by a square thin plastic case, Roberta turned it over. Having worked with coins, she immediately recognized this one. Her eyes grew large as she realized she held in her hand a 1933 Saint-Gaudens Gold Double Eagle, the most valuable coin in the world. One had sold at auction for $6.6 million in 2002.

She grasped the coin firmly in her hand and looked in awe towards the back of the bedraggled man who was still walking away. "Oh, my," faintly squeaked out of Roberta's mouth.

She thought, I wonder what Santa Claus wears when it's not December.

Two Place Poems

By
Barbara J. Bina

~~~~~~~~~~~~

Homeless Shelter

Pale
Decrepit
Abandoned
Hope
Having been worn down
Across the years
Inside its shell
Screaming silent words
Defying ultimate destruction

~~~~~~~~~~~~

My Birth House

Empty
Weatherworn
Ramshackle
Sadness
Missing precious families
In an abandoned field
Upon a lonely hill
Waiting for new owners
Watching them never arrive

A NEW LIFE

By
Barbara J. Bina

A pair of ravens fly
silently in the midnight sky,
watching the movement below.

Through their discerning eyes,
centuries can't disguise
that change is a continual flow.

When all lands were cold,
an ice crack would unfold
and let first people walk beyond a bridge.

To begin a new life,
a man helped his young wife
descend many a steep stony ridge.

When they reached level ground,
strange yellow flowers she found
and here they decided to stay.

Enmeshed in her fur cloth
hid a tiny gravid moth
which sadly could not fly away.

Several tribal groups fanned
throughout the new land,
hunted beasts and from others they'd hide.

The young couple was brave,
made their home in a cave.
The small moth laid her eggs and then died.

In time great glaciers bled
as mighty rivers fed
on the minerals, smooth stones and sand.

Ground previously frozen
blossomed new life when
grass, birch and willow burst from the land.

Moose and ptarmigan came.
Wolf and fox followed the same.
The hunter's tastes needed to change.

Birds migrated
as hungry grizzlies waited
for the caribou's return from their range.

Some people harvested grain
and chose to remain
stationary at ancestor's sites.

Others followed the herd,
left the land undisturbed,
tanning furs for the long winter's nights.

Now fossilized mammoth bones
lie silent near pingo cones
amidst ancient well-worn trails

Open to the few
who desire to start life anew,
and deal with whatever prevails.

A hopeful couple came forth
to travel far north
when circumstances asked them to dream.

Their cold hard journey was long.
Tired, he helped her along.
Pausing briefly next to a stream,

She cupped water in her hand,
saw yellow in the sand.
Overwhelmed they laughed till they cried.

Later on as they slept,
a small native moth crept
beside their tent, laid her eggs and then died.

A pair of ravens fly
silently in the midnight sky,
watching the movement below.

Through their discerning eyes,
centuries can't disguise
that change is a continual flow.

Edwards Brothers, Inc.
Thorofare, NJ USA
October 20, 2011